Everyday Heroes 3

*Another Collection of Inspirational and
Motivational Stories from Around the World*

Compiled By Matt Bacak

Edited by Jeanne Kolenda

ISBN-9798362044831

DEDICATION

Dedicated to the Heroes of tomorrow. Proceeds from this book
go directly to Habitat for Humanity.

ACKNOWLEDGMENTS

Thank you to all of the authors who shared their stories in this book, and a special thank you to Jeanne Kolenda, Stephanie Bacak, Zachary Maxwell, and Preston Rahn for your help in making this book a great success!

-Matt Bacak

INTRODUCTION

A hero is someone who is admired or idealized for courage, outstanding achievements, or noble qualities. A hero can be anyone – a friend, family member, teacher, or even a complete stranger.

Heroes come in all shapes and sizes. Some are famous, like athletes or celebrities. Others are everyday people who do extraordinary things, like firefighters or soldiers. No matter who they are, heroes make a difference in the lives of others.

What makes a person a hero? That's up for debate. Some people believe that heroes are born, not made. Others believe that anyone has the potential to be a hero if they put their mind to it.

One thing is for sure – heroes are an important part of our society.

They inspire us to be better people and to make the world a better place. Thank you, heroes, for everything you do!

Enjoy the book,

Matt Bacak

TABLE OF CONTENTS

7 Key Differences Between the Rich and the Poor

by Matt Bacak

People want to be rich for a variety of reasons.

Some people want to be rich so they can live a life of luxury and enjoy all the trappings that come with wealth.

Others want to be rich so they can help others, either by donating money to charitable causes or by using their influence to make positive changes in the world.

Still others simply want the security and peace of mind that comes with knowing you have a large amount of money in the bank.

Whatever the reason, there is no denying that wealth is something many people aspire to.

And while there is no surefire way to become a millionaire overnight, there are certain fundamental differences between the rich and the poor that you should know to increase your chances of achieving financial success...

Now if you look closely at the rich people we know, you'll likely find that most aren't particularly lucky, intelligent, or hardworking.

Let's take a closer look at some of the actual fundamental differences between the rich and the poor:

1. Rich people attempt to create a specific life for themselves; poor people believe they have no control.

If you don't believe you can create the life you desire, why would you even try? But if you can envision what you want, you stand a chance to get it.

2. Wealthy people dream much bigger.

Tell your poor friends that you want to be a millionaire and see what they say. You're likely to hear something like this, "No one needs that much money. You can live fine with a lot less than a million dollars."

* Do you think that a person who says things like this is ever likely to be wealthy? People who are poor always tend to think small. People who are rich dream big.

3. The rich play to win, and the poor play not to lose.

This is significant. The rich are quite bold and are always searching for a way to win when money is involved. The poor are too busy worrying about preserving what little they have.

They never give themselves the chance to become wealthy.

4. Opportunities vs. obstacles.

Those who are wealthy tend to focus on the opportunities and then simply deal with the obstacles as they arise along the way. The poor have a habit of focusing on all the obstacles.

* Focusing on problems makes it very difficult to find solutions. A problem-oriented mindset also can cause challenges in staying motivated. By keeping your eye on the prize and staying focused on solutions, you'll find continually moving forward to be much easier.

5. Commitment counts.

The rich do an excellent job at staying committed to achieving their goals. The poor are good at dedicating themselves to dreaming about their hopes instead of making goals out of them.

 * Although you may have fun thinking about how great it would be to be rich, that's not going to make your desires happen. Set a goal and then fully commit to it.

6. Peer group matters.

We all tend to rise or fall to the level of our peer group. Have you ever noticed that the rich hang out with other rich people? Spend time with wealthy people if you want to succeed financially. You'll be amazed at how your perspective changes when you hear people talking about how they made $2,000+ in a single day.

7. The rich constantly learn.

You'll find that wealthy people are usually learning new things, especially regarding making more money. The poor frequently have an attitude that they already know everything they need to know. Don't stop learning. Developing the habits and attitudes presented above will go a long way toward improving your financial situation.

It's never too late to start, and you'll be amazed at how quickly you can turn things around. Start today and you can change your financial life forever!

Meet The Author:

Matt Bacak is considered by many a Digital Marketing Legend. In fact, he was voted "Digital Marketing Legend of The Year" in 2019 and again in 2020. Using his stealth marketing techniques, he became a Best-Selling author with a huge fan base of over 1.2 million people in his niche as well as built multi-million-dollar companies.

After being crowned 2010 Internet Marketer of the Year, he was asked to appear on National Television and his Lifetime television segment focused on "How to make money using the Internet...the real way." Matt is not only a sought-after internet marketer but has also marketed for some of the world's top experts whose reputations would shrivel if their followers ever found out someone else coached them on their online marketing strategies.

13

Overcoming Curveballs

by Adam Baetu

Addiction.

Backstabbing.

Diabetes.

Heart Attack.

Covid.

Ice Skating Uphill and an 11-year journey into the light.

I don't know if I would ever classify myself as a hero.

I'm a bit of a liability most of the time.

I've been through the wringer a bit... But I have come out of the other side smelling mostly of roses rather than shit.

Here's what happened...

2011 - I was a very successful broker in the city of London, with some huge habits!

That February my Mum died unexpectedly from a brain hemorrhage... talk about a curveball!

It forced me to reevaluate my life - I just knew I had to do something more with my life.

I swear, when I decided to leave the city, Columbia entered its biggest economic crisis ever.

I had two beautiful baby boys that I just wasn't seeing and an amazing wife who had forgotten what I looked like.

I walked away from a fortune to save my life and my marriage.

Did I know what I was going to do? Not a clue.

Did I know anything about marketing? Nope.

Did I have the faintest of ideas that it would be how I'd end up making my next fortune?

15

Not A Clue.

I could do a few card tricks, so I started walking into pubs and restaurants working for tips...

It was hell. Trying to be nice and funny to a bunch of fat wankers in restaurants. I'm not a funny guy. And I struggle to be nice to nearly everyone I meet.

I met another dad while I was dropping my youngest off at nursery.

We started talking, and it turns out he had an "email marketing" business.

I didn't even know what email was at this stage. I had a Bloomberg account with a messenger thing that I used to send messages to other traders.

Email? WTF was that? And how on earth did you make money from it?

Funny though. Everyone assumes that because you work in the financial world, you're an amazing businessperson.

Ha... I didn't know how to run a biz... I knew how to get drunk and shout loudly...

But I digress... This fella asked me to run his business for him and since my diary wasn't exactly full, and my earnings weren't exactly, well, anything... I said YES!!

So that was me, discovering what email was and how it can be used for business.

I was on my way. My journey had begun.

We worked together building this awesome company until October 2014 when the dirty bastard tried to fuck me. Not literally. Financially. He showed his true colors and tried to get me ousted from the company I had helped build.

I found out about it and launched my "I'm taking what's mine, you fucker" undercover operation.

After some legal wrangling and bank account raiding, I ended up walking away with half of the value of the business that we had built.

So, I found myself on my own once again, building a business from scratch, and I'll never forget the day I got my first client for £150 per month to send emails out for him. It was a great day. Back then I used to advise clients to send out no more than one or two emails a month. How funny is that?

I ran and built that business until October 2020.

It was a good business. There were a few hiccups on the way. GDPR came along and blew everything out of the water for a little while. So, I started to learn how to run Facebook ads, and I got quite a few clients locally, nationally, and internationally. The business was going really well. I had a turnover of about $500k per year and pretty much zero overhead. No staff to worry about. The bills were being paid, and there was food on the table.

I got bored.

You see, when you're running an agency and doing work for other people, essentially, you're just the hired help. And I don't like being the hired help.

Increasingly, I came to the conclusion that most clients were a royal pain in the rear. Ninety percent of them didn't even know what they wanted, and the other ten percent knew exactly what they wanted but didn't have the budget for it and still expected the results that they thought they deserved.

It started to drive me around the bend, so I decided that rather than be the hired help, I would become the wizard instead.

I would become the consultant, the person who had all the knowledge that I could impart to these clients without actually ever having to do the work for them.

So, in October 2020, I decided to sack all of my clients and hang up my shingle as an online coach.

I landed my first client as a coach, and I was going to teach him how to run Facebook ads.

I landed that client without even having created the course that I was going to teach him. My plan was to actually record the sessions, use that as the course, and resell it to other people.

And then a couple of things happened in very quick succession. Life can really throw some lemons at you…

In February 2020 I was diagnosed with Type 2 Diabetes. I went on a fitness regime. I changed my diet. I changed my lifestyle, and I started to go out and do regular exercise, walking, running, and generally getting fit and starting to really take care of myself.

On April 2nd, 2020, I went out for a run, came home, felt chest pain, and had a heart attack. Oh, and did I mention that this was 13 days into the first UK Covid lockdown?

So, I found myself in Watford General Hospital, which at the time was known as "Covid Central," having a stent put into my arteries while everyone around me was dropping like flies from COVID-19.

It obviously put a slight dent in my plans of world domination as a coach.

I was laid up, recuperating, wondering how on earth I was going to earn a living. And I realized that I had to build a HUGE EMAIL LIST FAST.

I spent a few weeks testing different squeeze pages, lead magnets, and other methods and set about it like a demon on steroids, and built a new coaching biz completely from scratch.

If you're not getting the message yet...

THE POWER OF EMAIL!

I did manage to capitalize on the growing trend of online zoom sessions, and I built my client base. I spent a bit of time creating new courses, which I then sold via email to my growing list. Some were one-on-one training courses, some were online courses, and some were group training courses.

Having the skills and techniques to build lists meant that I could still earn during a pandemic, having had a heart attack and without ever having to go and deliver a "pitch."

Everything I did was based on email. EVERYTHING!

Around November 2021, it occurred to me that I could only sell my courses to my audience a certain number of times. There would start to be a repetitiveness that people would get bored with, and so I started to learn about how I could monetize my list in other ways.

And that led me to the world of affiliate marketing.

What a massive wild west mashup of rubbish affiliate marketing is.

There are so, so many "gurus" telling people what to do, using methods that just do not work.

I figured out pretty quickly that trying to sell $11 offers from Warrior+ was about as much fun as biting off someone else's toenails.

Other affiliate sites won't even payout for 6 months, and the entire ecosystem is full of scammers.

I woke up one morning to find that $1700 worth of sales of one of my products had been fake purchases with stolen credit cards that one of my "legitimate" affiliates had been using.

That brings us to today.

I have a wonderful coaching business and an awesome online business, and I complement all of that with affiliate offers that pay out proper commissions regularly.

I'm launching my next course in the new year. It's called Top Secret Affiliate, and in it, you can also learn how to build an affiliate marketing business that can pay you $5k, $10k, or even $20k per month from the comfort of your own laptop anywhere in the world.

>> You'll learn exactly how to build a hot email list of rabid buyers and how to get them to pay you commissions FAST!

>> Which affiliate sites to sign up for.

>> What affiliate offers are the best to promote.

>> And how to avoid all of the traps and pitfalls that make 90% of affiliate marketers fail.

You can get on the waitlist here >> https://www.topsecretaffiliate.com/

And for those that are on the list before the official launch, you will also get an exclusive discount on the launch price, plus some top-secret freebies that everyone else will wish they had!!

Meet The Author:

Hi, I'm Adam Baetu.

I'm well known for helping business owners grow their businesses online.

I've run and managed over 250,000 Facebook Ads. Sent over 1 million emails and spent and managed over $20m on paid advertising campaigns for myself and my clients.

I love seeing that "Aha!" moment on my students' faces when they realize how powerful lead gen and online sales techniques can be for growing their income.

I now concentrate most of my time creating accessible online courses and running group training sessions.

When You're Unsure - Just Tap into This...

by Devon Brown

"Devon. I need you to kill fifteen minutes."

The audience had come back from break and there were now over 350 people sitting in front of an empty stage. Waiting.

My boss, Matt, and I were backstage. I could see the wheels turning in his head as he paced back and forth with the microphone in his hand.

"15 minutes?!" I asked, thinking he had misspoken. "What do you want me to do for fifteen minutes?"

"I don't know," Matt said, the frustration in his voice obvious. "But the next speaker is running late and assuming he gets here at all, he won't be here for at least 15 minutes. So just kill as much time as you can!"

And with that, he handed me the mic and went off to figure out a backup plan just in case the guy who was supposed to be on stage didn't show.

"15 Minutes!" – I thought to myself. "That's a long-ass time. What the hell am I supposed to do for 15 minutes?"

During the 20-second walk to the front of the stage, I hoped my brain would provide an answer to that question. But nothing popped into my head.

If I had the knowledge and experience I have now, I could have easily come up with several things that would have worked in that situation. But at that point in my career... I did not have the two decades of experience on stage that I have now under my belt. Come to think of it, this was only the 3rd or 4th time I had ever emceed (hosted) an event.

I stood in front of the audience of hundreds, center stage, and nervously switched the microphone on. As if triggered by turning on the mic, something inside me whispered an answer.

"Devon, just dance hip-hop with them."

Had I had time to process how dumb the idea actually sounded, I probably would not have done it. But there was no time.

I just had to go with it. I brought the microphone to my mouth and said...

"Hey everyone. Before I bring the next speaker to the stage, I want to do a little exercise with you to get our energy up. What I need you all to do is stand up, and when the music starts playing, I need you to clap along with me."

I don't remember what song I asked the A/V guy to play or what dance I did. But as the song came on and the beat began to pound through the speakers, I motioned for the audience to clap along following my rhythm. Within moments, all 350 people were clapping in unison and the energy in the room had leveled up by 400%. As if on cue, the beat dropped, the chorus of the song began, and yours truly stopped clapping and broke out into a hip-hop dance routine. When I finished, the audience went from rhythmic clapping to cheering and applause.

It felt great, but I'd only killed about 3 minutes.

12 more minutes to go. I thought to myself.

What the hell was I gonna come up with next? "Was that fun?" I asked with a smile on my face, already knowing the answer given the positive glow in the room. "Now, as you just saw, I love to dance hip-hop. And while I've got a little time on stage, I need your help with something."

I continued, not exactly sure how the audience of mostly white male, baby-boomers (whom I assumed knew more about The Rolling Stones and Led Zeppelin than they did about MC Hammer, OutKast, and Missy Elliot) would react to the out-of-left-field words that were about to come out of the mouth of the 27- year-old black kid standing on stage in front of them...

"Now, I know you're here to learn about marketing your business on the internet, but I'm looking for some new members for my hip-hop crew, and I have a feeling that my new dance crew members are right here in this audience. So, while I'm not going to teach you all of the crazy nonsense I just did, I am going to teach you a little something. I want you to spread out and follow along with me."

They laughed.

I could tell that many of them thought I was joking because they began to sit back down.

"I know, I know..." I said, hands up with a big smile on my face. "You think I'm joking? But I really am going to teach you some hip-hop. I promise it will be fun, so just spread your arms out and make sure you're not too close to anyone... you know, just in case you've got exceptionally big dance moves, we don't want you accidentally dance-punching someone in the eye."

For the next few minutes, I led the crowd in a simplified version of the dance I'd just done on stage. The crowd – most of whom had never listened to, much less danced, hip-hop music – started following along with me. I taught them a simple series of hand movements called "tutting" - where you make a bunch of right-angles with your hands, so named because you look like King Tut walking like an Egyptian. Many seemed nervous at first, but by the second time through our mini-routine, most of them, to my surprise, were actually catching on really well.

As I finished teaching them the dance, I looked at my watch…. Dammit, still 6 minutes to kill… and I don't see Matt.

I commended them on their efforts and then asked them the next question that popped into my head: "Now…who wants to come on stage and do it with me?"

Their reaction was as if they were all reading from the same script. A hearty laugh and a shaking of the head as if to say, "Look here, Mr. Hip Hop… we had fun with you dancing as an audience, but there's no way in hell you're getting me on that stage."

But after a little coaxing… I managed to get six worthy participants on the stage. I had the guy at the AV booth turn the song back on and, with the rest of the crowd's support, we began.

With my new dance crew on stage and the crowd clapping along, we performed our tutting routine.

Was it perfect? Far from it.

But we were having fun.

And when we finished our not-so-on-rhythm rendition of hip-hop dancing and the crowd, smiling and laughing, had given us our applause, I turned to the audience.

"I have a confession to make." I told them - "I'm not actually looking for a dance crew. I honestly just wanted to see who would break outside of their comfort zone, come on stage, and do something you've never done before knowing full well that you'd probably mess it up. These six did. So, for that, they get a reward. Because that's the thing about life. Life isn't asking you to do it perfectly. Life is just asking you to have the courage to try. And when you say yes, even when it's scary, that's when you get the reward you weren't expecting."

I motioned for one of the event staff to bring me some free t-shirts, hats, and other gifts we had at the event, and I proceeded to let the brave souls on stage with me pick out multiple prizes.

23

The crowd cheered, and my new dance crew (ecstatic about their prizes), high-fived me as they left the stage. I looked to the back of the room. The guy who was supposed to speak had arrived, and Matt gave me the thumbs-up to let me know I didn't have to keep stalling.

As I left the stage, I got a standing ovation. That evening, after the event, several people sought me out to shake my hand and tell me that they'd never had so much fun at a seminar. They couldn't believe that I'd gotten the person they were there with to dance, and they expressed to me that my lesson about breaking outside of their comfort zones was the exact push they needed to enact the information they were learning at the event.

I was grateful for the compliments, but to be honest, I didn't think I had done anything special.

But I had.

I had given them the one thing they wanted from me and the one thing that life wants from YOU.

I had given them authenticity.

You see, if there was a step-by-step handbook for event emcees, I'm pretty sure you'd be hard-pressed to find the chapter that says, "If you have a crowd of mostly white guys born in the 1950s and 60s, and they're at the seminar to learn about internet entrepreneurship, then play rap music from the 2000s for them, and teach them a hip-hop dance battle routine".

I find it hilarious just writing those words because, on its face, it seems so stupid. But for me, it worked.

Why?

Because it was authentic.

AUTHENTICITY, and having the courage to live into it, is what allows you to tap into the unique magic that's inside you.

AUTHENTICITY is what connects us at a deep human (heart) level.

AUTHENTICITY is what enables you to live the truest, best, and highest version of yourself.

How can I say that?

Because once I realized that I could be my authentic self on stage - and that the crowd would love me for it - I was able to carve out a unique niche for myself. Today, as you read these words, I'm the world's #1 live event emcee. I've shared

24

the stage with people like Tony Robbins, Les Brown, Brian Tracy, Russell Brunson, Brendon Burchard, Rachel Hollis, Amy Porterfield, Dean Graziosi, and people from TV's Shark Tank (just to name a few).

But I never would have been able to achieve this success (or touch the number of lives I've touched) without first understanding that my authenticity was what was going to get me there.

So, my question for you is this...

Are you living into your most authentic self, or are there areas and places you're holding back because you THINK it's how you're "supposed" to be?

When I was unsure of what to do on stage, I tapped into my authenticity.

Luckily, I did not have the time to question what I was doing; otherwise, I might have missed out on the world of opportunity that comes when you lean into who you truly are.

So, if you are unsure of what next step to take, just tap into your authenticity. Figure out what action(s) you'd take if you were free from fear, judgment, or ego... and live into that!

Meet The Author:

Devon Brown is an entrepreneur and speaker and is widely regarded by many as the World's #1 Event Emcee.

For live events, seminars, and conferences, when the biggest names in personal development, entrepreneurship, internet marketing, fitness, and personal development need someone to excite and energize their audience, Devon gets the call. He's hosted events from Los Angeles to Singapore and has shared the stage with such greats as Tony Robbins, Rachel Hollis, Dean Graziosi, Brendon Burchard, Russell Brunson, & Les Brown. Once referred to as "what would happen if you combined MC Hammer, Ryan Seacrest, & Tony Robbins", Devon is one of the most fun and entertaining people you'll ever see on stage.

One Story You'll Never Forget!

By Dr. Ivan Carney

When my clients work with me, I try to give them ideas, strategies, and techniques that will double or triple their bottom-line income…if my ideas are implemented! One thing is for sure. They WORK!

If you're a presenter, a speaker, a marketer, a business owner, or an online businessperson, you're going to want to read this short chapter.

I'm going to tell you two stories you'll never forget.

The first one is a fascinating story I read the other day that I want to share with you.

It's about the late Moe Levine, a renowned lawyer who argued more than 2,000 civil jury trials. He was an exceptionally good litigator. One trial great, Rick Friedman, called Mr. Levine "the Shakespeare of trial advocacy."

So, here's Moe Levine's story.

Moe was representing a man who had lost both of his arms in a horrible, grizzly accident.

For his final closing argument, Moe decided to do a different close.

Instead of the long, drawn-out closing statement of that many attorneys use, Moe stood up, buttoned his suit, composed himself, walked over to the jury, and told them this simple story:

"As you know, about an hour ago we broke for lunch. I saw the bailiff come to you and take you away as a group to have lunch IN the jury room.

Then I saw the defense attorney, Mr. Horowitz, get up, grab his briefcase, and say something to his client about where they should go to eat. Then the judge and court clerk got up and left, and I assume they all went to lunch.

So, as everyone was leaving, I turned to my client, Harold, and said, "Harold, why don't you and I go to lunch together?"

Harold looked at me with this funny look and said, "Okay. Great. I would love to do that with you, Mr. Levine."

So, we looked around and decided we would go across the street to that quaint little restaurant at the corner and have lunch. We wanted something close, so when we came back, we wouldn't be fighting traffic. (Then there was a long pause by Mr. Levine.)

Then he said something the jurors never forgot, "Ladies and gentlemen, I just had lunch with my client. As you can see, he has no arms. At lunch, Harold had to eat like a dog because of this horrible, horrible accident." He paused after he said that, looked at every juror, and then said, "Thank you."

Then he sat down.

The jury was not out long.

They came back with a unanimous decision.

The jury awarded Levine's client, Harold, one of the largest settlements in New York state history.

WOW!!

The moral of the story is this. Tell the truth. Be authentic. State the facts and talk to people emotionally in everything you do.

Here's another story to illustrate why I do what I do.
I'm a Doctor of Chiropractic, a nutritionist, an acupuncturist, a writer, a copywriter, a marketer, and a father. I graduated from Palmer College of Chiropractic in 1983. By 1997 I had six clinics with twelve employees and was able to adjust up to 158 patients in a single day. Things have changed. I'm now semi-retired, but I could and would still adjust that many people if I needed to. I love what I do, and if you tell me to adjust 100 patients a day, I could do that with a smile on my face.

I've worked with some of the greatest marketers and copywriters in my lifetime, and I still enjoy working with people who are "action-takers."

In 2015 I met a doctor at an event who was doing real estate, mentoring on the side, had a side hustle of selling cars at his car lot, and was then doing some coaching with a few clients. As you can tell, he was a diverse doctor and had his fingers in a lot of stuff, but for some reason, he wasn't doing any chiropractic adjustments anymore. Why? I don't know.

What I found interesting about him was this: I told him I was going to have to drive two-three hours that evening to pick something up for the presenter in Menifee, CA. Once I told him this, he asked if he could drive me to pick those items up.

Remember. This was a two-hour drive, if not more, depending on the traffic on the freeway. Granted, gas prices were not what they are today, but it was his overwhelming care and grace that captured my attention.

He didn't ask for anything in return. No money for gas. Nothing.

He was cordial all the way. We had a wonderful time. He was easy to talk to, and when we arrived back at the Woodland Hills Marriott later that night, we

28

did what chiropractic doctors do. We adjusted each other.

The event was nine days long. When we were done, we both packed up and left.

I didn't talk to him from that point forward.

Three months later I got this phone call. It was from a number I had never seen

before. It was Dr. Paul calling me from his personal phone.

We exchanged greetings. Then he tells me he wants to send out a mailer to a group of 100 podiatrists, and he wants to know if I can do everything for him, including mailing it for him. He wants a done-for-you service.

I told him I could do that, but I asked him what he was going to teach podiatrists, how he was going to help them since he was a chiropractic doctor, what the costs were going to be per month for them, where they were going to schedule this event, what his hook was, and how soon he needed the mailer.

He tells me, "Dr. Carney. I want to do a three-day seminar, give them at least twelve ways they can make at least an extra $100,000.00 per month, then close them on working with me as their coach and consultant to do just that."

So, I thought about that for a moment, then I asked him, "So, Dr. Paul, are you

sure you can deliver? I want to produce something different for

them, but Paul, the HOOK has to work right out of the gate, or you will be wasting your time and money."

Dr. Paul says, "Listen. If I can get them in the room, it's not going to be a problem closing them. I give lots of great content; I have the templates and everything else they need to make that extra $100,000.00 per month, plus I

know how to do it. All I need from you is the direct mail piece. That's it. I need you to tell them the hotel is on me, the food is on me, and if they decide they are not a fit for my program, their airfare is on me."

I asked, "So what you're telling me is this. They can pay to come and if they are not satisfied, they can get their airfare, hotel, and food reimbursed. Is that what you're telling me? Are you sure you want to do this?"

Dr. Paul pauses on the phone, then responds by saying, "Doc, if you can create a direct mail piece to get them to Las Vegas, I'll hire you to create it. I know Joel brags about what you can do for people sending direct mail, so I'm in! Just tell me how much, and let's get started. I want this room to be full in Las Vegas in two months, and all I want to do is show up. You send them the mailers, you mail them, and I'll take the reservations. Make sense?"

I said, "Okay Dr. Paul. I'll call you next week. I have to talk to you next week, tell you what I have come up with, get your approval, order a few things to go inside the envelope when you give me the go-ahead, tell you how much it's going to cost to mail out the letters, do the mailer, and once you're onboard and you've paid me, we'll get it done in a couple of weeks."

He laughed and said, "I'm counting on you. Let's talk next week."

I did the mailer, and I don't want to talk about how I did it here. That's something I only share with my high-level clients, plus it would be lengthy if I wrote it out here, so I'm going to keep it to the results.

I wrote the five-letter sales page.

I created what I was going to put on the front side as well as the back side of the envelope.

I bought a transformation mechanism I put inside the envelope.

I went to Staples to buy a few items to go on the outside of the envelope, then I went to the post office, did a mock-up, found out how much the postage was going to be, bought the appropriate stamps, etc., and went to work to get it done.

The letter was the hardest thing to do. Yeah, I do emails that are out of this

world, get attention, and get opened, but that's not what he wanted. He wanted a direct mail piece that would 1) get opened, 2) get read, and 3) get people to respond quickly. That was it.

So, we only mailed out 100 pieces. He had a list of podiatrists he sent to me on an Excel sheet. I looked them over and they were from all over the country.

I sent out about 35 envelopes per day. I wanted to take two or three days to

stagger them so that he wouldn't be overwhelmed with bookings.

Did it work?

Yes, it did.

Reservations started coming in. And remember, I only sent out 100 invitations. In fact, I missed about ten of them so only 90 went out. I'm not sure what happened, but there were only 90 sent out.

67 responded and came to his three-day presentation. At the end, he made his presentation. How many of those doctors wanted Dr. Paul's coaching weekly in a group setting? 37. Yes, 37 doctors said, "I want you to coach me, Dr. Paul."

That meant Dr. Paul spent $10,000.00 for me to do this direct mail piece, which ended up making him $111,000/month for two years.

Remember the book "Acres of Diamonds."

Find out what you do best, and then find the people who want what you offer.

That's it.

Meet The Author:

Dr. Carney is a Marketing Strategist who has written books on direct response marketing, email marketing, lead generation and how to write your books in digital form so they get noticed, opened, read, and acted upon. He started his career as a marketer in 1983 when he started running newspaper ads for his Chiropractic clinic. After 10 years in practice and learning marketing from people like Dan Kennedy, Gary Halbert and Jay Abraham, he was seeing 158 people in a single day by himself.

He had a staff of seven assistants and loved helping people with all kinds of health conditions. He is a mentor, coach, and consultant to business owners, both online and offline, where he helps them to increase their profits, get more leads, and double or triple their growth. He's a speaker, trainer, marketer, writer, doctor, visionary and avid listener. He has traveled to Tokyo, Hong Kong, Malaysia, and other cities outside the US to talk about what he does, how he does it, and how anyone can get what they want if they're persistent, teachable, and ready to act.

If you would like to talk to me personally, you can contact me at:

https://bookandmoney.com/call

BONUS: If you schedule a call, I'll send you two links after the call. Those two links will go to 2 digital books I've created that will get you excited about writing books, and doing videos, and show you exactly how to get more qualified leads without spending any more money.

Smiling All the Way to The Bank

by Dr. Chase O. Dansie

I'm a hopeless lover of word jokes, or as my kids call them "Dad Jokes."

So, when it came to the title of this chapter, I couldn't help myself. One of the biggest things that keep us from smiling is not making enough money, and in many ways, it's the perception of not making enough money that drives our dissatisfaction. I am going to talk about two "banks" that you may or may not smile about when you think of them.

The first is a bank of a river.

When it comes to our personal wealth and freedom, it's like you're standing on the side of the bank of a river wondering how you're going to get to the other side. And on the other side is wealth, happiness, freedom, peace, and possibly an easier life. For some, it's retirement, vacation, or just being able to quit the job that you've been doing and not enjoying for all these years. There it is in the distance, waiting for you to somehow row your boat over and grab it.

The other bank is the actual bank, the financial institution.

You know, the bank you have the app for on your phone. It's the app that you wake up in the morning and open up to check and see how much money there is in your account. You're waiting to see if your paycheck ACH fell into the account, waiting to see if the credit card processor has deposited your sales from last week so you can pay your employees. You're waiting on the bank to tell you the funds are released from a hold.

Waiting. Always waiting there on the bank looking out over the water. Waiting for the bank to tell you it's okay. Waiting for that loan to come, waiting to be approved, waiting for underwriting, wondering if your credit score is good enough this week for the plans you have ahead. There you are, you find yourself waiting for someone else to tell you that it's time to be successful. It's the same feeling you have when you are waiting on the bank of the river, wondering how you will get across to the other side.

What keeps a man from taking money to the bank

I've had an enormous amount of satisfaction helping people in my orthodontic office, and I have helped many people change their lives for the better. One of the things that I enjoy the most is seeing a man change his life by investing five or six thousand dollars in a new smile. I have seen it over and over. Usually, he is brought into the office by a good woman he is married to and who loves him very much. She wants the best for him. She wants him to succeed. She wants him to be the best version of himself. She secretly pulls me aside when he is with my staff and tells me that he isn't confident in himself, and she hopes he will gain that confidence by having awesome straight teeth. (This literally happens to me regularly.) She knows that changing his smile will give him the confidence that he wants, but usually, he's just too proud to admit it. Thank goodness for all the good women in this world who support and love good men and want them to be the best they can be.

I've learned that it goes much deeper than that - that the confidence in a smile is only the first step to releasing the power within a man. You're making a man all that he can be and helping him truly smile from the inside out - what does that mean? Let's take him back to the bank – the financial institution.

He walks into the bank with his leather bag, or just with a folder in his hand, ready to sit down with the banker. He knows when he does, he's going to have to talk about the topic that makes him feel the most naked and unprepared as anything else in the world; how much money he makes. Even worse, he will reveal his net worth in the dreaded "personal financial statement." It's like feeling like you are in first grade again and being called down to the principal's office. But this time, the principal is weighing your value as a human not by whether you are tardy or have great citizenship but rather by if your assets outweigh your liabilities, and when those are fine, he harps on your cash flow problems. The banker principal can see right through him.

"Smiling all the way to the bank" is a modification I made from the saying "laughing all the way to the bank." When was the last time you laughed as you were driving to the bank? Maybe you made a transaction so significant in your life that while you were taking the check to deposit it, it brought a smile and laughter bubbling up within you.

What if this was something that we experienced every day? What if every day we had that wonderful feeling of laughing all the way to the bank, and it was just part of us? What if our confidence were going before us like a force field and we knew that no banker, no woman or man, nobody at all could stop us from getting what and where we want? What if standing on the bank of a river we could be so certain we will make it to the other side that we see it as if it were done already? We could make more money and be happy with our progress with all the other parts of our life we want to make better.

How can a man instantly boost his confidence and his bank account?

I have seen men instantly upon getting braces, have so much more confidence that they have immediate improvements in their business and sales lives.

An example is Gary, who shared his experience getting braces while he was a sales agent at Aflac. Aflac has a fantastic way of tracking and helping agents see their sales progress, so Gary knew how well he had performed before and after getting braces.

He told me that immediately after getting braces, he had a jump in his sales performance so significant that you could see it jump up on a chart from the software that tracked his sales and that it remained above that level ever since. Imagine permanently bumping your sales and revenue from a 1-hour procedure! As his confidence went up, so did his sales.

And sales kept growing, he gave increased appreciation for the way it felt to look at someone and smile, knowing that he wasn't being judged for his teeth. It's such an easy example to see how confidence in a smile can make a difference.

But what may be less visible is the lack of confidence that comes when you just don't feel like you're making enough money to do what you want. It may be enough for what you need or what the bank tells you that you are allowed to want. But it's not quite enough to have your wife kiss you the same when you come home and tell her you spent the money on your favorite hobby. When you're making just enough, those extra things you like to have and do just end up stressing her out. But when you make much more than enough, it is a non-issue to her and you. So, in many ways, the wife who wants her husband to become the most confident man in the world is rooting for him because it will make it easy to be happy supporting him in his hobbies and the things he does to keep himself living his dreams.

Newly found capabilities arise from the most painful experiences

A crisis and one of the biggest challenges of my life hit me extremely hard suddenly. I spent 11 years in college and came out with two doctorate degrees, first becoming a successful dentist and then specializing in orthodontics. For 10 years, I built a successful orthodontic office and made a lot of money changing people's lives through orthodontics. I was also working out and I looked great. My biceps were filling out my shirt sleeves and my quads filled my pants as I had never experienced before. I was really feeling good about myself, and my confidence was soaring.

But one day, after being in my best health, I suddenly developed a really severe pain in my upper back; then I got a broken rib, then a painful SI joint, and then my feet developed plantar fasciitis pain, making it so I could hardly walk when I got up out of bed in the morning. For the reader who has experienced plantar fasciitis, you know what I'm talking about -you just sit there and hope that the pain will pass and you'll be able to walk again. I was actually crawling out of bed straight onto my hands and knees and crawling across my house to the garage to go to work. But the problems did not stop there. One by one, every joint in my body began to have problems. Ankles, fingers, wrists, shoulders, neck, jaw, hips, knees . . .

You name it and it was painful, and I found myself barely able to get up and go to work each day. But a miracle happened each day, one that I attribute to the power of God, and I was able to work through the terrible pain. It was at that time that two important things happened that have changed my life since.

I decided to be the master of my mind. And through an amazing combination of mental exercises and painful physical tests, I learned how to become the master of myself. I say that first because sometimes people focus on money so much they fail to realize where the true source of change comes from. The source of change is right in your mind. I learned a pathway to success that has allowed me to break through, and now I teach it to others.

The second result is that I decided to try something new. I was already highly successful in the way that I had been making money. Orthodontics and teeth were something I knew very well and my bank was very excited about it. When it comes to orthodontics, I didn't feel like I was on the side of the river waiting to cross. I felt like I was already there. I am very capable of success there.

But with a new challenge of physical incapacity, I quickly realized how important it would be for me to be smiling to the bank in ways that did not require all my joints to work. And this is where my capability bloomed in affiliate marketing, business coaching, and personal coaching. What I do now is help people get from one side of the river to the other, to get to the "bank" on the other side and get more money in their "bank" accounts. It happens first in their minds, and then you start to see it manifest in their bodies (including teeth and smiling) and every other aspect of life. This newfound confidence gives them more joy in life, more success in marriage, parenting, business, and greater financial freedom. It begins with admitting you aren't already where you are trying to go and recognizing what you are most capable of inside.

Meet The Author:

Dr. Chase Dansie is an orthodontist turned author, consultant, and online marketer. He grew up as an entertainer, performing for tens of thousands of tourists from all over the world in his family's business at Bryce Canyon National Park in southern Utah. Each night, he and his family's team made visitors to their show laugh and smile as they were taken on a covered-wagon ride through the forest simulating the "dangerous" Wild West and were treated to a show and dance featuring western music with his family's band.

Since his years entertaining tourists, Dr. Dansie has found multiple other ways to bring a smile to people's faces and excellence to customer service in business. As a talented orthodontist, he and his team not only light up people's lives with straight, white teeth but focus on the things that build their lives inward and help them have meaning and purpose in life. His online programs help people develop their personal skills and have the right mindset for challenges in life and business.

His podcast "People that make me smile" is centered around the everyday people who are heroes to him and especially those who have overcome or currently face some of life's difficult challenges with optimism.

Dr. Dansie's goal is that, because of his work, people all over the world will get up in the morning, walk in the bathroom, look in the mirror, and smile because they have more confidence in their capabilities, have better relationships with others, make more money, have better-looking smiles, and a greater confidence in their businesses.

You can learn more about Dr. Dansie, his online programs, books, private coaching, podcast, and orthodontic office services at drchasedansie.com

How To Reach the Masses and Achieve Your Dreams - My Top Publicity Tips After Scoring $5.8 Million in Free Advertising from The Media

by Ron Douglas

My heart was racing at what seemed to be a million beats per second as the producer whispered to me "Get ready Ron, you're going to be on right after this next segment." I couldn't help but think about all the people watching and all the family and friends who were looking on. Some root for me and others just analyze and judge my every move.

"What is she going to ask me?" I wondered with great anticipation as the butterflies swirled around my stomach.

"Ron, 30 seconds," the producer said.

For a moment, I was frozen by the thought that I might embarrass myself. I knew this was an opportunity that would open exciting new doors for me. I realized that I was finally getting the exposure that I had wanted. But at that moment, I wished I would have just said NO. Why did I agree to this? What if I say the wrong thing? Oh my God, I'm freaking out...

Then, one thought crossed my mind that finally calmed me down at just the right time. It was a quote that I had on my wall at home:

"To every man there comes in his lifetime that special moment when he is figuratively tapped on the shoulder and offered a chance to do a very special thing, unique to him and fitted to his talents; what a tragedy if that moment finds him unprepared or unqualified for that which would be his finest hour."

~~Winston Churchill

The point is, if you want success badly enough, your opportunity will surely come, but you have to be ready for it.

In the end, I went out there for my first television interview to promote my "America's Most Wanted Recipes" cookbook on Fox News and I did just fine. I knew my story and my topic better than any television host could. Once I started talking about it, the nervousness went away, and it was just a simple conversation. I went out there and did what I had to do.

Success is like that pretty girl who smiles at you but waits for you to make the first move. To win her heart, you're going to have to step out of your comfort zone. You're going to have to rise to the occasion and grab the success you deserve.

Practically everyone has a potential story in them that is press-worthy. If you have a product or service that's good enough for customers to buy, there is an angle you can find to get publicity. The media has to constantly find new stories to cover. Just looking at some of the nonsense that gets featured every day should motivate you.

So, what's stopping you from doing it?

It all starts with believing in yourself and taking the first step.

Ten Surefire Ways to Guarantee You Get Publicity

1. Leverage a current hot story.

The media is always looking for expert opinions on current events that are getting a lot of buzz. If you can release your opinion as an expert on topics related to a hot story, there's a good chance you could be asked for an interview. The key to this strategy is having credibility as an expert and acting fast.

2. Associate your story with something that's already famous.

The media knows that people are always interested in news related to famous people or things. If you can come up with an interesting spin for a story involving something famous, the media will be knocking down your door.

3. Correct a common belief.

For example, when the BP oil disaster in the Gulf Coast was still a hot story, the common belief was that the environmental damage had spread and ruined the beaches. This really hurt the hotel and tourist businesses in the region.

Savvy businesspeople in Destin, Florida, and other areas were able to get lots of publicity for their businesses by providing video updates of the beaches and showing that they were still safe to enjoy.

4. Dispel a myth to create controversy.

Everyone knows that the media loves controversy because it commands attention and sells. A sure way to stir up some controversy is to dispel a common myth - especially if people feel strongly about it.

Almost every industry produces myths. As an expert in your industry, you have the inside information to dispel those myths.

For example, if you're an expert on diet and nutrition, you could dispel the myth that low-carb or low-calorie diets actually work. You can show evidence that people on those diets gained back all the weight and use that to get exposure for your own, more balanced diet plan.

5. Tap into a fear that people have.

The press sees its role as serving the public and is keen to jump on a story if there is some type of risk or danger involved. Fear is one of the greatest motivators that command attention.

For example, someone selling a home security-related product can put out a story showing how there has been an increase in burglaries due to the economic recession and what you can do to avoid it happening to you.

6. Solve a common problem that people have.

People are always looking for easy solutions to their problems - especially problems related to important needs like health, safety, and financial security. If you can position your press release as a practical solution to an important problem, you have a good chance of getting coverage.

For example, right now lots of people are having a difficult time selling their homes in this tough real estate market. You could provide a solution with a product or service that helps people sell their houses quickly and for the highest price possible.

7. Use calendar events.

The media loves to do stories related to holidays or important anniversaries - Thanksgiving, Christmas, New Year's, Valentine's Day, Halloween, the start of the school year, the tax deadline, the anniversary of Elvis' death, the anniversary of the 911 tragedy, etc. If you can create an angle that ties your story into the current calendar event, you can get publicity.

For example, on Christmas, you can do something good for an accident victim who recently made the news. An act of goodwill and generosity to someone less fortunate allows you to get publicity by doing something good.

8. Do something extreme.

Sail around the world, jog across the country, jump out of an airplane for charity, break a world record, etc. - the media loves to cover extreme things that aren't frequently seen.

9. Start a 30-Day Challenge or Event.

Events that the public would be interested in make good stories in the media. Especially when you can tie it into an existing story and it helps people in some way.

For example, right now many people are unemployed and having a tough time finding a job. If you sell a product related to finding a job (resume writing, interviewing, etc.) you could get exposure for your business by hosting a "30-Day Find-a-Job Challenge" in which you would spend 30 days helping people for free.

10. Target industry-specific or local stories.

People focus on getting mainstream national coverage, but it's often much easier to get local or industry-specific publicity. You can tap into the important news related to your community or your industry and associate your story with that.

For example, if you own a pizza shop and a strike or lockout is going on at a local industrial plant, you could support the workers by offering free pizza for them at a certain time of the day. This would attract members of the local media who are covering the story.

Tips for Writing Effective Press Releases

1. Make sure your story is newsworthy. It has to be interesting and something that people want to know about.

2. Include a headline that commands attention and motivates the reader to keep reading.

3. Get to the point and keep it brief. Don't ramble. Press releases are typically less than one page.

4. Review some examples of successful press releases and follow the same format.

5. Start with a brief summary of the news, and then expand on who distributed it and why.

6. Address the facts and try to include real numbers and stats where applicable.

7. Provide all your contact information, including contact name, title, email, phone number, fax number, address, etc.

8. Avoid excessive use of adjectives and overly demonstrative language. Keep it business-like and don't appear too biased.

9. The goal of the press release is to sell the story and not a product or service. If your press release appears just to be a sales pitch, it will be ignored.

10. Use up to two quotes in the press release from the representative of the company or entity that the press release is about. Including more than two quotes is not recommended.

The process of getting publicity is often a gradual one. You can start out small and build your way up. Begin with the local newspapers, trade magazines, and radio stations to build up your resume of appearances. Then, use those interviews to get even more publicity.

Don't just depend on online press releases to reach media contacts. Do your research to find physical addresses, fax numbers, and even phone numbers to follow up. If you don't have the time to do it yourself, consider hiring an assistant or an outside publicist. If you do hire a publicist, be sure to check references and avoid signing any long-term contracts.

Once you've established yourself as a credible source to interview, you'll be more able to score larger publicity opportunities.

The point is that you have to take the first step and get started. Hopefully learning from my experience has motivated you to do just that. Good luck.

Meet The Author:

Ron Douglas is the president of Automated Profits, a digital marketing company established in 2001 which has produced multiple 7-figure brands generating over $35M in sales.

As an entrepreneur for over 20 years, Ron is widely known as one of the foremost experts in information publishing, webinar selling, and event marketing.

Ron is also the New York Times Best Selling Author of the "America's Most Wanted Recipes" cookbook series which has sold over 1.5 million copies and been featured live on Good Morning America, Home Shopping Network, Fox and Friends, NBC News, and in People Magazine.

Ron holds an MBA in Finance & Investments, is a Chartered Financial Analyst (CFA), and has worked on Wall Street for J.P. Morgan and Citibank. However, in 2007 he left a promising career and 6-figure job to work from home and spend more time with his kids.

Today Ron enjoys helping students worldwide use the internet to earn more, work less, and have a greater impact through his online programs and events like WebinarCon, the #1 mastermind event for Webinar Marketers.

The Rug Was Pulled... Now What?

By Richard Fedrizzi

In the movie *Forrest Gump, Forrest said a line that has been twisted and turned around many times; however, it goes something like this "My Mama Always Said Life Was Like a Box of Chocolates. You Never Know What You're Going to Get."

Well, That's pretty much an accurate statement.

Let me tell you a true story to illustrate this point.

A young man was looking to improve his employment situation.

You see, he was newly married, and they were expecting their first child shortly.

After numerous interviews, he accepted an entry-level management position with a Fortune 500 Aerospace company. He intended to stay and learn from this company, then within 5 years move on to a different company for a better position and money.

His new position with this company was overseeing a depot location, which included a packaging operation, shipping & receiving operation, GFM (Government Furnished Material) operation, finished goods quality inspection, and buy-off. He would also interface with government and foreign representations.

Most of the time, it was simply understanding and ensuring contractual requirements were met.

As time progressed, the regional headquarters vice president reached out and wanted a one-on-one meeting with him. To the young man's surprise, the meeting went very well. Apparently, some of the government & foreign representatives spoke highly of him and his support.

During this meeting, the VP arranged for him to meet with the regional director of logistics.

Shortly after starting this new position, the young man became involved with the IT/software team at the depot. They were trying to develop software that would automate the final inspection and buy-off process.

After including the government and foreign representatives, they succeeded and received an authorization letter from the local contract government office.

As a result, it reduced the number of processing days after buy-off and billing from 120 to 30 days.

During the meeting with the VP of logistics, several improvement topics were discussed. As a result of this meeting, the director asked him to head up a new department for estimating container and shipping costs on government deliverable products.

This area was costing the company tremendous amounts of contract overruns. And they needed a way to control it.

Working with the package engineers, contract, finance, and a lot of documentation, a process was developed for estimating packaging costs. During the first contract pricing audit, the government audit team challenged packaging costs. However, after a two-day review of the process and detailed pricing costs. The new estimating method was approved, saving necessary overruns.

His career progressed within the company, and he was promoted to a project manager position. Some of the major accomplishments included: the expansion of the shipping software, establishment of the packaging cost estimate process, development of an import/export software, a manufacturing critical material order process, implementation of an RFID (Radio Frequency Identification) process, and exploring the functionality of using IOT (Internet of Things) within the manufacturing process. (IOT refers to the collective network of connected devices and the technology that interfaces with applications.) All projects were implemented company wide. And each represented major cost savings to the company.

His plan of only staying 5 years stretched into 35 years.

Then in 2019, the COVID-19 pandemic arrived and sent the world into a panic. COVID-19 had a major impact on people, the way we would conduct daily business, and a financial impact.

As a result of COVID-19 and the financial impact on businesses' bottom lines, substantial changes were implemented. They were small at first; however, larger ones followed.

He received a call early on a Monday morning. It was the regional and human resources manager. His department was being eliminated, and all projects would transfer to Texas Headquarters. This was their two-week notice... After 35 years of service, it all ended in a 10-minute call.

The above illustration is a true account of events.
And that young person was ME...

Within 10 minutes, not only did my life take a hard left turn, but so did the lives of the folks that reported to me.

The looming question was, now what do I do, how do I replace my income?

I started to look around the marketplace for employment opportunities. However, because of the pandemic, opportunities were slim, and businesses were not hiring.

I remembered back in 2013, I dabbled a little with the Internet, I even made a little money from it. So why not give it try again? But it had changed from 2013 to 2020.

I need to make a list of elements I would need to get back on the internet to hit the road running and make some money.

My list included items such as:

Programs, applications

Email List, what type

Niche (whatever that was, I had no clue)

Costs

Potential income

Realization of why and expectations

The first issue I addressed was the WHY. Why I am doing this and my expectations. I thought to myself, "I got this!" But it wasn't until I wrote them out that I really knew my Why.

My ways included:

Replacement of my yearly income

Ensure all expenses/ bills were covered

Medical costs were covered

Home maintenance costs covered

Not to worry about spending time with my family and children

Now that I had my WHY figured out, I needed to address income.

Again, just saying replace my income didn't cut it. I needed to be very detailed about it. I started with a copy of my pay stub - what was itemized on it.

Medical, taxes, 401 contributions, Social Security, etc. Then I looked at my household expenses, mortgage, property taxes, utilities, vehicle loans and maintenance, household expenses, etc.

I broke down what I needed to make daily, weekly, monthly, and yearly. I was surprised at the numbers. But this is where your WHY comes into play. It helps to put everything into perspective.

I then printed out the Why and monthly targets, and I posted them next to my computer. I also kept a copy in my wallet. I read them two and three times every day. It helped to keep me focused.

What training would I need and what type was available? I had to do some research. What program or applications were needed for me to start on the internet and generate income? If you google "how to get started with affiliate marketing," there are a ton of programs. The trick is trying to decipher which were legitimate vs scams. Also known as shiny objects.

Believe me, there are a lot of them promising the moon, and you're making your first $1000 within 24 hrs. It's not that way. You need to put some time and effort into whatever program you select.

So don't waste your time and money chasing shiny objects.

One common item each of the programs had in common was an email list. I discovered there are several types of email lists. The most important is a buyer's list. These are the people that have purchased from you and look forward to your email. If they purchased from you once, they would likely purchase again. You don't need to have a really big list; you need a qualified buyers list. In fact, a buyers list of 200 – 500 is more valuable than a list of 100,000 non-qualified buyers.

After understanding the basic principles and how affiliate marketing worked, I started to focus on three types of programs, which all centered around building a buyers list.

List building

Email formatting

Traffic sources

I found mentors or experts in each of these three areas. It will not be easy for you. However, there is one way to tell if you have the right expert. Listen to what they're teaching you and watch what they produce. If they practice what they teach and it's working, you have a winner.

Follow their techniques, tips, and examples. But remember, you want to make them your own. Put a little bit of yourself or your flair in each email or sales page you put out. Your customer will notice this and relate to you. It will not be immediate, but if you mail every day, you'll start to see the difference in your open and click-through rates.

When I started to work on my email list, which was only 90 people, most were family, friends, and a few people from solo ads. This list was built back in 2013, and at that time, I didn't know what to do with it. I hardly ever mailed to it. For all intents and purposes, this list was dead. I had to either put new life into it or start from scratch. Bringing a dead list to life again is possible; however, for 90 people, it was better to let them rest and start fresh.

I will admit starting a list from scratch is not easy; however, if you follow your mentors' instructions, examples, etc., It won't be long before you start growing an active list. (Tip: A fast way to grow your list with zero cost to you... Look around for "Giveaway Campaigns." They're simple to join, and all you do is post a gift. The gift could be anything, a report, eBook, service, or program. All you do is mail your customers, offering them 100s of free gifts. They go to the site, look through all the gifts, and when they select yours, you get their email address. Now, remember, there will be hundreds of other people mailing to the giveaway site. So, your list could grow by a few or hundreds of email addresses. In either case, that's more than you had before. These giveaway campaigns are going on all the time. Just rinse and repeat.) I use this method often.

As you build your list, start making sales and hitting the affiliate leaderboards. You'll start to get noticed by the top affiliate. Then some magic will happen. Affiliates will start contacting you to promote their products.

Keep in mind that when you see your first sale from email marketing, whether it's $1, $7, or $10, it's going to feel like you hit a million-dollar jackpot. You'll remember that feeling for a long, long time. You'll also want to share that win with your spouse, family, or anyone who will listen. But don't worry, the odd look you may get from them is simply because they don't know the amount of effort, struggles, and long hours you put in to get that sale.

Now that you have that first $1, you can repeat it and multiply it. But you can't multiply $0s... You can multiply $1s...

I've gone from an income being taken away to building my own income that I control and will not be taken away.

You can succeed and do the same.

*Forrest Gump registered to Paramount Pictures

Meet The Author:

Richard Fedrizzi was an infantry Army Captain, a Peace Officer with the City of Los Angeles, and a qualified award-winning small and large bore marksman. Degrees from: California State University of Long Beach, University of La Vern, Georgia Institute of Technology. A retired Aerospace Project Manager.

An established entrepreneur since 2013. Published four children's books, (for ages 4 – 8), Internet List Building Book (Traffic from Scratch), and a self-help book

(Magellan Effect). Visit: https://rdtrinity.com

Get Someone on Your Side

By Reed Floren

Matt asked me to write a follow-up chapter because he liked my chapter "Blaze Your Own Trail" in Everyday Heroes 2.

Inside this new chapter, you'll discover some of my new favorite methods and tools I use to experience success my

life and in my business.

Get someone on your side

Entrepreneurship can be lonely, and you will become filled with self-doubt. You must find someone in your life who can be your cheerleader.

That person could be a coach/mentor, your spouse/partner, a parent, a close friend, a sibling, or even a loyal dog who does its best to cheer you up.

Ideally, you'll want as many as possible on your side.

A coach/mentor can help you avoid pitfalls, and you will achieve success faster.

A spouse or partner who supports you, making your home life better.

If you are lucky enough to still have your parents, cherish them.

A supportive friend who can help you when you're feeling down.

If you've got siblings, and they support your dream, that's fantastic, and it's a relationship that lasts a lifetime.

We're lucky enough to have two fur babies, and they always give me a good mental break by wanting to go on walks or play.

I often talk to the dogs throughout the day, and it feels great.

Invest in yourself.

It's never too late to put some money into a retirement account.

They won't give you a loan for retirement like they did to go to college, buy a car, or purchase a house.

It's up to you to fund your retirement, and even pennies you invest today can be big dollars in retirement.

Speaking of people, money aside, set up a health savings account.

Healthcare is expensive, and you can save a lot of money on taxes and let your health savings account grow tax-free, so take advantage of it.

We spend a third of our lives sleeping, and so many people neglect the power of sleep.

Get yourself a high-quality mattress, and blackout curtains, eliminate blue light sources (TV, cell phone, computer, tablet, etc.) an hour before going to bed, and get into a routine of 8 hours of sleep a night.

Invest in education that you can implement and see a result.

I have eliminated a ton of sources of "noise" by focusing on getting a lot of my knowledge from two places this past year.
#1 - Optimize.me (https://www.heroic.us/optimize) They have broken down 600+ of the very best books to give you the core wisdom inside, plus they have 50+ hour-long courses and over 1,000 micro courses, and it's all FREE!
#2 - I really like Rich Schefren's Steal Our Winners.
(https://www.richschefren.com/steal-our-winners

It's like getting two brand-new courses each week that you can easily implement and start seeing results.

Twice a week, Rich interviews a marketing expert, and they break down a new method that is working like gangbusters for them.

He gives you a video, audio, transcript, and the action step you need to take to implement the winning strategy.

Success is all about who you know.

Live events are the easiest way to meet others.

Get away from your computer, leave the comfort of your home, and press the flesh.

Your life & business will change by going to events and befriending other entrepreneurs.

Don't know of any marketing events? Check out Muncheye's live event page (https://muncheye.com/events.)

Be accountable

The only thing that matters is EXECUTING so you can get RESULTS.

Being accountable to others is the best way to execute more.

The thing that I really enjoyed about joining Matt's Secret Email Mastermind was that he wanted us to join an accountability group of three other marketers. Tim, Charlene, and Dave :) I hope you enjoy this chapter. You've had a major impact on my life.

Every Monday, we open up a spreadsheet and write the answers to:

"What is your goal?"

"What did you do this week?"

"What did you do well?"

"What do you want to improve?"

"What tasks are you doing this upcoming week?"

Then we all hop on a Zoom call and spend 15-20 minutes each going into more detail on these answers, and the rest of us help each other with our blind spots and motivation to reach the next level.

We've recently added a Shelper (https://www.shelper.com). This is a real person (Hi Shelly) who runs a group text message with us.

Each day we share our to-dos and what we want to focus on.

Shelly then checks in with us throughout the day and gives us that extra nudge to check off those items.

To come up with my to-do list, I break down what I'm focusing on inside our accountability group and then use a free tool called Google Keep (https://keep.google.com/) to write my to-dos.

What's beautiful about Google Keep is that it's web-based and accessible from all my devices from my computer to iPad, to phone, to Apple Watch, to E-ink Tablet... making it easy to check off to-dos from anywhere.

Biohacking and gadgets for fun & profit

2022 was the year for me to really dive into biohacking.

If you aren't familiar with biohacking, it has really picked up steam in the last few years, especially in the entrepreneur space.

You might wonder what biohacking is.

Biohacking is optimizing your mind & body through alternative means whether it be micro dosing drugs like LSD, using electrical stimulation, or even something as simple as spicing up your coffee with grass-fed butter.

People all over the world are experimenting with improving their performance through biohacking.

I'm not interested in experimenting with drugs, but when I went to the Consumer Electronics Show (CES), I saw this device people were wearing on their necks called a Hapbee (Hapbee.com).

The Hapbee simulates the molecular interactions that different chemicals like caffeine, alcohol, melatonin, CBD, nicotine, etc. have on your brain without the side effects.

It's one of those devices that you see and think "Oh this is totally a scam," but I have to let you know when I have it in sleep mode, I'm more rested and have more vivid dreams.

When it's set to focus, I get a ton more done.

And when I have it set to a blend of alcohol, I'm way more outgoing and giddier talking to people.

What I really like about the Hapbee is that it lets you experiment with how chemicals impact your mind & body without having to ingest anything.

Another gadget that I used to really get going is called the Apollo Neuro (https://apolloneuro.com)

The Apollo Neuro looks like an ankle monitor but is really a stress relief wearable that uses vibrations at different speeds to help you wake up, be more outgoing, get clear & focused, rebuild & recover, meditate, relax and unwind.

You can feel when the Apollo Neuro changes modes, and I find it to have a near-instantaneous impact on my mood.

Have you ever struggled with bad habits?

I have a Pavlok (https://pavlok.com) that you wear on your wrist like a watch.

Pavlok helps you be more mindful, and focus, and replace bad habits with good ones.

How does it work?

Pavlok zaps you when you do a habit you're trying to break. The shock is similar in strength to snapping your wrist with a rubber band, so you will not get hurt.

Do you need a fast way to de-stress?

The Calmigo (https://Calmigo.com) uses 4 of your senses: vision (feedback lights), hearing (vibrates), smell (calming scents), and touch (how the device feels in your hand).

Calmigo rapidly decreases your stress levels in as little as 3 minutes, and I have found it to be a useful tool when I'm in a bad or anxious mood.

Touchpoint (https://thetouchpointsolution.com) is another vibration gadget I wear on my wrist, which promises to increase focus, reduce stress, and improve sleep.

The downside is you need to wear it on both wrists and the vibration can make an annoying sound compared to my other gadgets.

Block distractions on your electronics. Freedom.to is my favorite tool for this.

With Pomodoro Technique, you select one task to focus on for 25 minutes and get as much down as possible, take a quick break of 5-10 minutes, and repeat with another task. After 4 Pomodoro sessions, take a longer break of 20-30 minutes and then repeat.

If you live in an area that gets cold, invest in a heated vest/jacket. You'll feel fantastic, and they are great conversation starters.

A heated eye massage is a great way to start and end your day. I use a Renpho Eye Massager (https://renpho.com/collections/eye-massage).

Sleep Score Max (https://www.sleepscore.com/sleepscore-max-sleep-tracker/) is a very accurate sleep tracker that has helped me improve my sleep. They also have a free app, so you can try it out before committing to the physical device.

3M™ Micropore™ Surgical Tape is what I used to tape my mouth shut at night, which helps improve the quality of sleep and can lessen the effects of snoring and sleep apnea.

AIRMAX Nasal Dilator helps prevent snoring and increases oxygen to your lungs by 76.1%, making it easier to breathe and helping you sleep.

As someone who uses computers a lot, I have found blue light-blocking glasses to reduce eye strain and help me sleep better. Studies show they decrease the risk of macular degeneration, which my mom suffers from.

As I get older, I'm getting more worried about losing my hair, so I purchased a red & blue LED therapy light you wear under your hat, and it's supposed to help your hair grow.

I found it on Alibaba for $40.

Does it work?

It's too early to know for sure, but the good feelings of trying to prevent hair loss have been well worth it.

I live in Minnesota and suffer from depression.

The cold dark winters really bug me, so a Seasonal Affective Disorder (SAD) therapy light has helped with my mood.

An Under the Desk Elliptical can help you burn calories while at your desk or even watching shows.

Speaking of desks, they say that sitting is the new smoking. Invest in a standing desk so you aren't always sitting on your butt all day.

Put multiple monitors on your desk so you can follow along with training and implement without going back and forth on the same screen.

Another useful desk accessory is a Stream deck (https://www.elgato.com/en/stream-deck), which allows you to optimize your workflow, and let your computer get stuff done with the press of a button.

If you have a treadmill, you might be interested in getting a treadmill desk attachment to get some work done while you walk.

Bionic Gym (BionicGym.com) feels super gimmicky, but it gets my heart rate going and I'm very sweaty after doing it. It makes your thigh muscles rapidly contract just like you would if you were shivering. In response, your heart beats harder and faster, and you can even get a runner's high while wearing it.

Ultiself (Ultiself.com) is a fantastic website and app that helps you "never miss a day" of your habits by using checkboxes and gamification.

AI & The Future of Digital Marketing

Artificial Intelligence (AI) has crept into our lives, and I expect to see more and more uses for it.

Tools like Jasper.ai and Riku.ai can create your marketing content.

Tools like CheatLayer.com, which uses AI to help you automate tasks and also create software solutions you can sell.

Otter.ai or Spoke.app for transcripts and then popping those into WordTune Read (https://app.wordtune.com/read). Providing these AI notes has been a powerful way to network at live events.

Each day more and more tools like these are released, and it's very exciting to see new technology coming out to make us more money.

Meet The Author:

Reed Floren has been marketing online since 1999 when he was only 13 years old. He has spoken about digital marketing on stages in eight different countries and has helped thousands of people achieve success. You can discover more about Reed here:

https://www.imreviewandbonus.com/

Your Children Can Be Your Heroes

By Tracy Grote

One of the most powerful things any person can do is raise a child. Whether they are a genetically related child or one from another family, a child is a life-long commitment regardless of their age.

There is a well-known saying that to have a child is to wear your heart forever outside your body. Think teenage angst was painful? It's nothing compared to the first time you have to deal with your own child's heartbreak.

We get preoccupied with ensuring our children have the essentials, such as food, shelter, and education and we forget much of what our children need is for us to impart a spark of desire in them to succeed and reach their full potential.

As parents, we hope our children surpass our way of life in terms of education, financial security, and standard of living. We anticipate that our children will learn from our mistakes and other life lessons as they face everyday challenges.

For a child to have an opportunity to be a successful adult, their childhood

experiences should instill in them that they are successful. It doesn't have to cost thousands of dollars in private school fees or extra-curricular activities. Spending time listening and in conversation with your child can create bonds that last forever.

The other day, my oldest child reminded me of what I shared with her over 25 years ago when she felt overwhelmed with middle school homework. She recalled it felt like she had the weight of an elephant on her. My response was that while it might seem overwhelming, if she "ate" the elephant one bite at a

time, there would eventually be no more elephants. She learned to break down her homework assignments one task at a time, which enabled her not only to be successful at focusing on one assignment at a time but also allowed her to excel in her studying methods and receive outstanding grades.

How Do We Define Success?

We, of course, want our children to be successful and grow up to be healthy, happy, and independent adults. However, we enjoy it when our children occasionally reach out to us for advice.

Children's education comes in many forms. We often teach them through our actions in solving problems and dealing with others. Regardless of age, children are like sponges.

They remember how you speak and interact with coworkers, family, friends, the people in the store, and the person behind the counter. Children observe and learn how their parents exhibit honesty, sharing, and caring in many ways for neighbors, friends, and family.

Parents should want their children to understand that success is not just about earning the most money. It is about awakening their child's dreams and hopes for their life. An important lesson is that happiness grows from a job well done and from giving others our gifts of time of love.

Our children will mimic our behaviors, but they are not carbon copies of us, nor do we want them to be. They may choose another field of study, a different profession, or a different place to live. They may decide they prefer a different type of family than the one in which they grew up. My daughters didn't choose to work in the real estate world I chose many years ago, but the work ethics they learned by working in my real estate office has enabled them to have very successful careers. The oldest daughter is a highly successful and well-respected leader at one of the larger railroad companies in America. My younger daughter chose to pursue a nursing career and is now a registered nurse working on a transplant team that saves lives.

Their successes have been possible by their ability to effectively work and communicate with a wide variety of people. The excellent skills they developed in identifying problems, managing a situation, partnering with different individuals, leadership, and communicating have enabled them to be able to problem-solve issues that arise within a variety of work settings. This combination is a winning formula for success.

What Don't Children Need

I was not the perfect parent. Like most other parents, I was short-tempered at times and on occasion, responded negatively to incidents. I was unable to attend every sporting event in which they participated. But my children understood that despite some of my imperfections in parenting, my love for them was steadfast – regardless of what they did that angered me. Having experienced their parents' behaviors and parenting styles, my daughters decided on how they prefer to parent their children.

Luxury items were not a necessary part of our life. Our children had many friends who lived in more expensive houses, drove new luxury vehicles, and wore designer clothes. But my daughters grew up in a safe, happy, and loving home and experienced simple pleasures like picnics, wading in the river, attending outdoor events like musicals and fireworks, exploring the ranch, and setting alarms to wake up for a moon eclipse; this made many special moments.

Through the years, they learned that extravagance doesn't always make for happiness and being content in life.

This is great news for parents who worry about how a lack of finances could negatively impact their child. It shouldn't. The saying 'necessity is the mother of invention' is certainly true when it comes to children developing creative and inquiring minds.

What They Do Need

Children are not born as empty vessels waiting to be filled. Every child has innate talents and a personality that will develop independently. As we watched our daughters grow, we quickly realized how they developed into very unique people despite only a two-year age difference.

They were given space and time to develop their special talents, and at the same time, they were given boundaries, a dependable home life with routines, rules, and responsibilities.

BOUNDARIES

Boundaries provide children with the guideposts needed for growing up to be responsible and ethical adults. Teenagers typically hate boundaries, but they later understand that respecting boundaries is critical in becoming adults in a world that must enforce boundaries. The developing childhood years are an important time to understand how to live within societal boundaries.

They also learn that parental love is steadfast and unconditional. Children must continually see evidence that regardless of the poor choices they make and the failures they endure, their parents still love them. Different children require different parenting strategies, but love is the basis for every decision and is

there despite the child's behavior.

Consequences follow poor choices and failure to respect boundaries. These include cleaning up a mess they created or apologizing to someone for something they have done wrong. Basically speaking, this boils down to respect for themselves, respect for others, and respect for things.

ROUTINES

Routines help fulfill a child's most basic needs; feeling confident they can rely on their parents to take care of them regarding food, sleep, shelter, or health and knowing that someone is there to care for them.

RULES

While children dislike rules, these are boundaries that they know if broken will result in various consequences. Our family didn't have a lot of rules, keeping the rules simple and consistent developed their sense of respect and responsibility.

RESPONSIBILITY

Children don't learn responsibility when their parents perform many activities for them. When parents become busy and find themselves running from activity to activity and balancing work and home life, they often move into the "I'll do it, it's easier" mode. Although it is challenging to set expectations and to ensure follow-through for children to clean their rooms, choose the clothes they wear, pack their own bags, and complete their homework, children develop a sense of responsibility and independence by performing these activities.

Provide Education

One of the best gifts given to our children was the desire to learn new things and develop. This not only included formal education but learning to pay attention to what was happening in their daily lives. They learned how current events and weather impacted their daily lives, such as what clothes to wear to school and what items to pack for a special trip.

While schools can educate children about history, geography, science, math, and literature, children also develop a keen insight into how to work together on a group project when some team members are not as devoted to the assignment and others are more driven to contribute. This desire to be surrounded by others who have a similar work ethic and desire for success has contributed to our daughters' professional success and recognition by their peers.

The Power of Role Models

Consistently modeling the behaviors we expect our children to learn is critical. "Do as I say not as I do" teaches children that they say one thing but behave differently. Telling our children that stealing is wrong while taking something from a store shelf without paying for it demonstrates a conflict.

Our children will never be exactly like us. We assume they will have the same drive, and passion and make the same decisions as we would in every situation. Some of their decisions may be quite different from ours. It doesn't make their decision "wrong." Understanding what we consider to be "right" and what they consider "right" can be quite different depending upon the individual's

perspective. 'Letting go' and respecting your child's decisions is important; they

will learn important lessons as they live with the outcomes of their decisions.

Social Skills

An individual's IQ used to be an important measurement of our ability to learn and retain concepts. It was something we were born with and developed with education and a positive home environment

Exposing children to a variety of learning opportunities such as music, art, sports, dance, and martial arts is often valuable in identifying a child's special gifts and aptitudes. Efforts and money spent on exposure to many opportunities and to develop their skills in something enable them to excel, feel proud of their success, and develop positive self-esteem.

Developing social skills is critical. Parents who display positive social skills give their children an opportunity to see these in real life. Children learn how to interact with others. Manners are developed and honed by watching parents and by practicing those manners until they become habits. All children need to learn to interact with a variety of people so they can use these skills later in life and interact with society as a whole. Respect for others is another key skill to develop.

Money, Money, Money

Providing education regarding money management is a key to success. Start small, such as earning an allowance for performing a task at home.

Encourage your child to use the money wisely after it has accrued rather than frivolous spending. Demonstrate the responsibility of saving money for something they may want later.

Do not buy children everything they want. Giving toys or games as rewards for hard work or having them earn extra money for an extraordinary job teaches them the lessons of receiving rewards for work performed and earning respect for the efforts of working.

The earlier you can teach your child to make money in a way outside of their salary or wage-earning method the better. Talk to your children about passive income and provide them ways to learn how they can earn it. I have found this instrumental in my adult years, wishing I had incorporated these alternatives earlier.

Elizabeth and Laura have been a joy in my life and watching them grow into the women they are today is a true reflection of their parents' engagement in their lives. T parenting skills are a testament to their upbringing, and they make us proud. Spending quality time with your children is the greatest gift you can give them. It is a precious commodity to cherish. While there have been many heroes and mentors in my life, my proudest moments are observing my daughters grow into the women they are and MY heroes they have become.

Meet The Author:

Tracy Grote was raised in the small hill country town of Mason, Texas. His parents instilled in him a strong work ethic. While growing up he not only worked on the ranch the family has owned since 1876, but also worked in his grandfather's garage. After obtaining an undergraduate degree from Tarleton State University and a Master's degree from Texas A&M University, he began a real estate career that has spanned over 45 years appraising millions, if not billions, of dollars in real estate.

His latest challenge and goal in life is now beginning as he learns internet marketing from the greats like Matt Bacak, Caleb O'Dowd, and Adam Baetu. While the need to be successful is paramount, so is the desire to succeed in order to donate to various groups, provide to those less fortunate as well as mentor family members to also become successful. To mentor and give back is the new goal.

Blockchain 101

by Mark Hartmann

You are probably wondering, "What is Blockchain?"

At its simplest, a blockchain is a digital ledger of transactions.

When a transaction occurs, it is recorded on a "block" which is then added to the end of the "chain," creating an immutable record of all past transactions. This record is public and transparent, meaning anyone can view it at any time.

This may not sound particularly revolutionary or exciting, but the implications of this technology are far-reaching.

By removing the need for third-party intermediaries (such as banks or governments) to verify and approve transactions, blockchain has the potential to fundamentally disrupt many industries.

How Does Blockchain Work?

As mentioned above, blockchain is simply a digital ledger of transactions. However, there are a few key features that make blockchain different from other ledgers.

First, blockchain is decentralized, meaning it is not managed by any one central authority. Instead, it is distributed across a network of computers known as "nodes."

This decentralized structure makes it incredibly difficult for anyone to tamper with or alter the data stored on the blockchain.

Secondly, blockchain is immutable, meaning once a transaction is recorded on the blockchain, it cannot be changed or removed. This provides a high level of security and transparency, as all past transactions are publicly available and verifiable.

Finally, blockchain is programmable, meaning that certain conditions can be attached to transactions. For example, a payment could be released only after a certain amount of time has passed or only if certain conditions are met. This opens up a whole new world of possibilities for how transactions can be conducted and verified.

Why Should We Pay Attention to Blockchain?

There are a few reasons why blockchain is generating so much excitement and interest from both the business and tech communities.

As mentioned above, blockchain has the potential to disrupt many industries by removing the need for third-party intermediaries.

This could lead to faster, cheaper, and more secure transactions across a wide range of industries.

Blockchain is still in its early stages of development and there is a lot of room for innovation. New applications and use cases for blockchain are being discovered all the time, and we can only imagine what will be possible in the future as the technology continues to evolve.

Finally, blockchain is a very hot topic right now, and there is a lot of investment pouring into this space. This is leading to rapid development and progress, which means we are likely to see even more exciting advancements in the near future.

So, there you have it! A brief introduction to blockchain and why it is something you should be paying attention to.

With so much potential for disruption and innovation, it is definitely an area worth keeping an eye on!

Meet The Author:

Mark Hartman is an author, engineer, and mathematician who is looking into the future of the significance of the digital economy and understanding how the digital economies will change the world of finances using the global arbitrage value of electricity as the unit of currency.

Mark is doing something exciting for you. At the time this publishing, he is gathering demo data to create a bonus chapter for you, when its complete it will be here: https://everydayheroesbook.com/hartman

10 Things I've Learned from The Entertainment Industry That Can Help You in Your Industry

By Nat Hecht

The entertainment business could be described as quirky, and while at times that might be an accurate portrayal, misconceptions about the entertainment industry abound. There is quite a bit of passion involved in the pursuit of creativity, and along with that creativity come high-octane emotions. Mix that up with tabloid gossip, and we have the perfect recipe for all those headlines and the resultant promotion, good or bad. The reality, of course, is less fantastic. In so many ways, the entertainment business is like many other businesses, and most of the things I've learned working in it can apply to any business. I've been attached to this industry in some capacity for my entire career, about 40 years now. In that time, I've discovered some pearls of wisdom that I believe could help others encountering challenges in their own careers in any industry, as the lessons learned are pretty much universal. Here are some observations I have gleaned that I think might help, in no particular order.

1. Everyone wants to be treated like a rock star, so don't let them down

While this might fall into the category of vanity, deep down inside nearly everyone wants to be the center of attention, especially if they are a client or a customer. If you think about it, on some basic level, your job is to cater to the needs of that person because you're working in support of their efforts and goals. In that role, your job is to not only provide the information and products for the task at hand, but it is also to make sure they are the center point of your attention and communication.

2. Don't Wear a Necktie If You Are Going to A Business Meeting in A Recording Studio

Know the culture adhered to at the company you're visiting and abide by the norms of the environment in which you're doing business. In years past, this adage would be seemingly obvious, but dress codes have been relaxed over time in many industries, and it is important to do some research in order to not show up and look out of place, or even offensive, to some of the people you're going to see. You've heard the saying "Don't judge a book by its cover"? Well, even in the publishing industry people do just that, especially now that we barely have any bookstores, and everyone buys their books online or reads them electronically on a device. It is a picture of the cover both on the shelf and online that sells the book in many circumstances, and despite the lesson to the contrary, and right or wrong, people all over the world tend to judge other people by the way they look before they know the content of their mind.

Another old adage, "You never get a second chance to make a first impression" comes to mind here. Once you are seen for the first time, that impression will always be the thing that sticks out in the mind of the people you meet. There is a certain recording studio owner I know of who hates neckties, and whenever anyone who isn't a customer enters the studio with a tie, he jumps up from his desk with a set of dress shears and cuts it off right under the knot. That's the last time you make that mistake! Don't be caught off guard – always be groomed and dress your best for that business meeting, and there will be one less thing to get in the way of gaining your customer's respect and ultimately closing the deal.

3.   Often the biggest stars are the most humble and down to earth.

It is easy to get nervous when meeting someone who is very important or someone that is a personal hero or a well-known person. A good thought to keep in mind in these situations is that many of these people were once in the same position as you are, they were on their way up, had mentors and professionals they respected in their career path, and are pretty normal and down to earth people as a whole. I've heard the horror stories, and maybe I've just been lucky, but every single famous person I have met in the entertainment industry has been nice, cordial, and respectful when I've met with them, at least so far. I've found that if you are offering a service or solving a problem for them to make their lives easier, you are already on a good footing while meeting with them, so it's important to recognize that and calm yourself. When you realize that you are there for their advantage, meeting them is just a fringe benefit.

It is often people who are not the big stars who try to intimidate and belittle others in their presence for a whole host of reasons. Stay Calm!

Kind of a corollary for the advice in #3 above - you will run into people who are just not interested in dealing with you on a personable level. In order to feel as though they are in control of the situation, some people need to let you know who the boss is, and sometimes it can get downright nasty. These individuals may be angry for any number of reasons. Maybe they had a bad morning, weekend, quarter, etc., and just need to let you know that they think you're one of the little people that are there to serve their needs and, as such, you should be happy that they're doing you a favor. It just might be that they have inferiority issues and are always one step away from being exposed as lacking, so they strike first. No matter what the reason may be, you are not their armchair psychiatrist! The best thing to do is to stay calm and focused on why you are there in the first place and recognize that no matter how difficult the situation may be, it is almost never about you personally. Once you begin to turn the subject matter of the conversation over to the reason for the meeting, things will move away from the unpleasantness.

4.   Don't assume that your unique ideas will be welcomed with open arms.

There are lots of great ideas out there. If you've thought of one and are excited about it, expressing it could be contagious with your customer or your superiors, and it could even result in a big sale, promotion, raise, or special recognition. It is important to express these ideas, but it is also important to be prepared if your idea might not be welcome. This can happen because of small-mindedness, but it also happens if your customer or superior has "heard it all before," doesn't agree with your unique idea, and wants to ride you for days until you agree with them that your idea was a bad one in the first place. You may feel that you have a better perspective because you're in the trenches with customers and listen to their needs, and it might be that your superior is not in touch with new trends in the market and is out of focus with your ideas. Maybe your boss or the customer just always has to be right. The important thing is to not be discouraged by this kind of response. Don't let the fear of rejection stop you from expressing your good ideas and keep track of them because you can circle back around to them in the future or use them if your situation changes within your company. If your ideas are rejected, keep them in your back pocket; they might work well at a different company or with a different customer as you move up the ladder if your current company or customer isn't receptive.

5.   Be your own best advocate.

Sometimes self-promotion is the only way others in your organization will understand what you do, who you are, and what you're capable of doing. Once you are hired for a job, no one really looks at your resume much. It is usually a loss for the company, in that most people have a larger skill set than the job for which they were hired. If your goal is to move up the ranks, it is important to toot your own horn and let the people you work with in on what skills you can contribute that are outside of your current job description. Once, after a casual conversation with a colleague who was known for being an electronics designer, I found out that he also had a decent knowledge of computer programming. In a twist of fate, I was aware of another one of my colleagues who needed a programmer immediately due to someone walking off his project. I was able to connect the two of them and the problem was quickly solved. If I had not begun a discussion about their background with each of them, neither would have known to talk to the other about their past experience. You never know from which direction your next career move will come, and if you can show you are highly skilled in different needed areas, you will have more opportunities.

6. Entertain all opportunities that come your way.

Going along with being your own best advocate is the idea of being on the lookout. Opportunities may come your way in the strangest of situations, so no matter where they come from, even if doing so might ruffle feathers or is "against" the rules, consider everything, and don't put up walls when an opportunity comes knocking.

Always be prepared before you meet with a customer; we all know that being prepared and doing the research necessary to answer your customer's question is important, but inevitably you will run into a question for which you just don't have an answer. When that happens, be honest with your customer and tell them you don't have an answer but let them know you will get the answer to the question and get back to them with that answer. This is far better than trying to provide an answer that is either wrong or just a supposition. Doing this will build their trust in you because you're being truthful in showing them your limitations, and it also shows your professionalism and that you kept your word in following up. It is always better to be in a position to help solve your client's problems via information they can use before asking for the sale.

7. Know your personal boundaries - Don't let anyone take advantage of your good nature.

It can feel like a huge personal affront when you discover that someone is trying to take advantage of you or denigrate your reputation. There are few things you can do to prevent or stop it from happening, other than having a really thick skin and a healthy sense of self-confidence, but here is some good advice about how to deal with difficult situations that sometimes crop up. First, don't let anyone take advantage of your good nature. Learn how to sidestep the people in your professional life who try to stand in your way, belittle you, or bad mouth you behind your back. No matter how good a person you are, at some time in your professional life, you may meet someone who just plain doesn't like you. It is usually easy to identify who these people are and to avoid them, but it is much more difficult to identify those who are hiding their true feelings behind a façade of pleasantries and smiles. Who knows what it is that these people are triggered by; maybe it is jealousy, fear of being shown up by you somehow, or that you remind them of a bully they hated in elementary school. The key point is that whatever it is, none of the reasons have anything to do with you. People who behave like this have a flaw in their character, and it happens between their ears, not yours. Don't let it bother you, just step around them and continue on your path. At least once in my professional life, I discovered that an individual who acted like a friend to my face was actually bad-mouthing me to management behind my back.

I stopped acknowledging that person from the moment I learned about it without looking back. In another instance, I discovered that one of the colleagues I had on my list of references I would provide on request to potential new employers was giving me negative feedback. Off the list they went. Don't let the bastards get you down!

8. Are you stoked about what you are doing in your industry?

Being excited about what you're doing in your position and bringing your passion for your work to every interaction with your customer and your coworkers will create excitement. Excitement can be contagious, so bring your passion for your profession and the knowledge you have to your meetings with customers and coworkers and show it in your other communications. Be detail-oriented and bring your "A" game to everything you do. If you can accomplish this task, you will not only be noticed and praised by your customers, leaders, and peers, but you'll feel an overwhelming sense of self-worth. Follow the advice of Zig Ziglar's well-known mantra: "You will get all you want in life if you help enough other people get what they want."

Meet The Author:

Nathaniel "Nat" Hecht has been a Pro Audio industry professional for 40 years. He started his first company called Audible Sound while attending Tufts University Engineering in Massachusetts, where in his senior year he was the recipient of the first ever Paul & Elizabeth Montle Prize for Entrepreneurial Achievement for his work with Audible Sound.

Eventually moving to Los Angeles, Nat began working for manufacturers building products for the sound reinforcement, recording industry, broadcast, and sound contracting industries, holding positions at industry leading companies such as JBL Professional, Sennheiser USA, Harman International and Bose Corporation. Nat held positions that ranged from Applications Engineering, Product Development and Product Management to National Sales & Marketing. An avid writer, Nat spent five years as the Editor-in-Chief of the international trade magazine Sound & Video Contractor, which won a Silver Ozzie Award for outstanding artwork during his tenure, and best new feature for a newly developed news blog called "S&VC Extra."

After the magazine Nat spent some time as an industry consultant to Pro Audio industry manufacturers. Currently Nat has been building e-commerce businesses in industries as diverse as leisure sports, health and wellness, and camping and survival. "There is literally a revolution happening on the Internet; those in the know are calling it the Golden Age of Online Business," says Hecht, "Online commerce has changed the way we all consume products, and it is an exciting time to be developing online businesses as opportunities online grow in leaps and bounds." You can contact Nat Hecht on LinkedIn at: https://www.linkedin.com/in/nathecht/

In the universe, there are things that are known

and things that are unknown,

And in between... There are doors.

~~William Blake

Knocking on Doors
[Life Lessons from Affiliate Marketing]

By Dr. Kate Hughes

As a kid growing up in a small Australian town, I loved to explore how things worked. When I was 3 years old, I found a marvelous thing. If I knocked on the front door of my house, my mother would answer. Over time her mood would shift from playing a game with me to being annoyed – to sometimes being really annoyed. One day, after knocking repeatedly and the door being answered, I decided that the game was not that much fun after all.

I was playing on the front lawn of our house when the postman came with a parcel to deliver. He asked if my mother was home. I said "Yes" and tried to tell him not to knock on the door. He laughed, patted me on the head, walked up the driveway - and knocked on the front door! No answer, and he knocked, no answer, and he knocked… until the door was opened with my mother yelling about how she was tired of me knocking and "if she opened the door that I had better watch out!" Embarrassing for her, quite amusing for the postman - whom she apologized to profusely - and very funny for me, at least at first.

I know there's a saying that "When one door closes, a window will open." But I don't want to climb out a window or just look at the view. I want to walk through doors, moving from what I know to the unknown, and increase the number of open doors in my life.

The journey to being a successful affiliate marketer is challenging, interesting, new, and just like your normal life, it is a messy process, and there are always more things to be done. I think part of the challenge is that it is a virtual system, and another part is that it brings together so many different skills and knowledge.

In my experience, affiliate marketing has challenged me in the same areas that "life" challenges me. You will find it to be the same. Are you a perfectionist? That will be there in affiliate marketing. Are you a procrastinator? That will be there too. Do you have to work hard to understand things, and THEN it all falls into place? Or are you a fast learner – yet slow to implement? These things will be there too. Then there's the issue that affiliate marketing is not a quick "cash cow" solution to finances – or life. How disappointing is that?

The Most Important Affiliate Marketing Tool

I've found that the most important "tool" for an affiliate marketer is not an autoresponder or a Facebook account or even amazing offers. It's persistence. This is needed in everything in life: to change a habit; to learn something new; to keep life balanced; to be an entrepreneur. However, as life gets busy, it's not necessarily persistence that leads to success, but it's persistence with a focus that leads to results. Many times, just "enduring" is mistaken for persistence. Many times, "playing" at something is mistaken for persistence. How many times have I heard people ask if I have a business that is making money – or just an expensive hobby? So, affiliate marketing needs to make money, and this will happen as the business develops.

Focus on the Outcome

I found there needs to be a focus on my persistence with my business.
What outcome do I want? If I just want "any" outcome, then I will get it. It can be success or failure or more of the same – each of those is an outcome. BUT if I want a specific type of outcome, then I need to persist, focus – and ask great questions.

When I first heard that I needed to "ask good questions," I struggled with that concept and kept asking myself: "How do I ask good questions?" and "What are good questions?" However, I found that in order to ask good questions, I first needed to think and just start asking questions. Over time they became good questions. I know that they are good questions from the results I am getting. Good questions give me focus on the business and help me solve problems.

Problem Solver - And not an entrepreneur

Everywhere I turn in my affiliate marketing journey and my entrepreneurial business, I face problems, issues, and challenges. "Oh no... NOT again." I used to share with a couple of friends in an informal Mastermind what my problems were this week. My friends would then share their problems, and we would sign off from the Zoom call with a sense of "Wow, so glad I don't have that problem!" or "My problems are more (bigger, better, stronger, or greater) than their problems." It was a badge of honor... but nothing changed. My business did not improve – and my fellow Mastermind friends' businesses did not improve either.

Until one day, we decided to take a different approach and change our perspective. We agreed that we were not business owners anymore, and we were not entrepreneurs; we were problem solvers.

This change re-framed everything. We now challenge each other to share how we solved a problem; and if we don't have a solution ourselves, we brainstorm together to find one, or several, potential solutions. This was awkward at first, but over time we're getting better at it, and we now, more often, encourage each other to grow and find solutions. This contrasts strongly with our old approach of just complaining about the (figuratively) closed doors in our affiliate marketing journey.

Outcomes With Measurable Results

Things started to change when I worked on my business "problems" and kept reviewing the results I was getting. Having data is so important (everyone says this), and yet I need to take time to analyze that information to determine how to improve my business.

Affiliate marketing is similar to constantly walking through different doors, moving from the known to the unknown. It's like walking down a long corridor with hundreds of doors and knocking on them as I walk by. Some doors open, and some don't; these doors are like opportunities, and I don't want too many to open at once. And I need to keep walking.

Opportunity "Knocks"

A really important lesson I have learned from the affiliate marketing process is that just because I "can" do something, it doesn't mean that I "should" do it. It all goes back to opportunities - and to be honest there are just so many of them. This is commonly talked about in affiliate marketing, this "shiny object" syndrome. Too many opportunities (open doors) and I get distracted. So, I don't shut down my curiosity and explore new things... I watch as a spectator and try to learn something new that I can apply back to my business and strengthen the results. I don't chase all the opportunities (nor buy all of the products), as I need to focus.

Most people stay with what they know. However, if you decide to be an affiliate marketer – or are an affiliate marketer – you have chosen to move from the known to the unknown. There are so many opportunities, and to be successful, you need to focus and decide which outcome you are pursuing. It takes time to succeed and good timing to get impressive results. Hang in there.

Go on, be courageous. Knock on those doors.

Meet The Author:

Dr. Kate Hughes is an expert in business systems and has helped numerous international companies to "understand the voice of the customer" over the past 20 years. Dr Kate holds an MBA and PhD in Business Strategy and Supply Chain Management and has worked with a number of business universities in Australia, USA and Europe. She remains active in writing and peer review of business journal articles.

Having guided companies in successful implementation of business projects, Dr Kate has set up her own affiliate marketing company to promote products in the Make Money Online sector and also works as an affiliate manager. She offers mentoring and coaching services for affiliate marketers who want to improve their business using proven world class business strategies.

Reach out to Dr Kate if you are interested in getting in contact:

Email: kate.hughes@key226.com

Subject Line: Everyday Heroes 3

The Shiny Trap

by Jeremy Kennedy

It was 11 years ago when I first found my way out of the daily grind, we call the rat race. After doing construction, truck driving, retail, food service, telemarketing, and a myriad of other non-optimal career choices, it was obvious that holding a job wasn't my forte. I was good at them, but I hated them.

I felt the call of entrepreneurship my whole life, but I just couldn't put my finger on what kind of business I wanted to run. At the age of 29, with a wife, a newborn, and another soon on the way, I knew something had to change. Like many others, I found myself scouring the internet late at night searching for any hint of a way out. One night I stumbled across a popular discussion forum on the topic of how to make money on the internet. I was instantly hooked.

There were endless threads of people discussing various methods that were making them gobs of money, all from their computers. I dug my heels in and tried method after method. I mean, I really went to town learning everything I could. But for some reason, I just couldn't make it work. I had found what seemed like the holy grail of money-making knowledge, but I was literally overwhelmed... It all sounded so easy but in practice, I just couldn't put the puzzle together.

After months of consuming nearly everything I could get my hands on, I was ready to give up. Then I came across a thread that completely changed my life. This guy had made over a million dollars that year selling these little info products on the forum. It hit me like a ton of bricks. I spent all this time BUYING every product under the sun and I failed to see I needed to be the one SELLING them. I've seen so many people fall into the same trap. We get so hooked on all the shiny little methods, tricks, hacks, and "systems" that we are completely blinded by what a "business" actually is and does.

If you take a birds-eye view, it's quite simple. Essentially there are three main parts. A business creates or obtains a product or service to offer. They get that product in front of as many people as they can (traffic). Once they have a customer, they offer them MORE stuff. That little formula is a way to print as much money as you'd like.

Given that you actually do provide what you promise, you can make different tweaks that can grow your business to almost any level.

Now, when I had that realization over a decade ago, everything changed.

At the time I had been playing around with an online social platform that is now defunct, but it was hot stuff at the time.

I wasn't anything close to an expert on it, and I really had no clue what I was doing. I had a couple of ideas of how a business could use the platform in a few unique ways, and that was good enough for me.

So, I sat down, fired up Microsoft Word, and wrote a very plain and ugly 20-ish page document about it.

Nothing fancy.

Then I wrote in another document maybe the worst sales letter ever written.

I had no clue about copywriting. I just mimicked what I saw other guys do in my niche.

After half a weekend of work, I put it up for sale.

Granted, I expected it to totally flop and by today's standards, it did.

I only sold 25 copies.

I didn't even know what an upsell was.

These days I would cry if I only sold 25 copies of a product.

But that day I made $300 from those 25 sales.... And I was ECSTATIC!!!

It would take me a whole week at my day job to make what I was able to do in just a day.

I knew right then and there I had found it. I finally found my way out.

I was trading "things" for money instead of my time.

About a week later, I quit my job.

I wouldn't recommend that to a budding entrepreneur, but I KNEW if I did it once, I could do it again, and I haven't had a job ever since.

For the past 11 years, I've done the exact same thing. It's generated over 7- figures and afforded me the ability to comfortably take care of my family.

I've stuck to the same formula.

Create SIMPLE products that get a result.

Add my customers to lists (Email, Facebook Groups, YouTube, SMS, etc.).

Offer more stuff to the customers on my lists.

The list is ultra-important.

If you just sell a product and say goodbye, you constantly have to find more customers just to survive.

But building a "list" of customers allows you to send communication to your customers at any time, on-demand, for years.

I can write an email now, send it to my list, and within the next few minutes watch sales start pouring into my account for the rest of the evening.

That's the power of a list. That is real "push-button-money."

I have customers on my list who bought my very first product over a decade ago, and they still buy from me today.

It's easy to see how that is nothing short of life changing.

I also owe a BIG huge fat thank you to Matt Bacak for three incredibly valuable life-altering lessons he taught me after being my mentor for a year.

#1 – He taught me how to get out of the "roller coaster."

That is, the spikes and drops from releasing a product, making a windfall of cash, and then it dropping till you do it again (the email list does help mitigate this by promoting other businesses' offers in between).

The trick is simple, RECURRING INCOME.

He taught me that when you add a monthly recurring offer to your business, you create a consistent, reliable, truly job-replacing income stream.

I now have hundreds and hundreds of people paying me across multiple recurring offers that add thousands each month to my bottom line.

It's truly a beautiful thing.

#2 – I asked him one day why I was stuck at 6-figures.

His answer was so simple, but it smacked me right across the face. I almost felt stupid at how simple it was, but the way he framed it just really changed everything.

He said, "all your crap is too cheap; you don't charge enough, and you don't have anything over $1,000."

He continued "How many units of a $1,000 offer do you need to sell this year to make $1 million bucks?"

Only 1,000... in an entire YEAR.

This was when I could sell 1,000 units of something in like 2 DAYS, let alone a year.

"What if it was a $2,000 offer?"

You only need to sell 500... only FIVE HUNDRED and you've made a million bucks.

I was flabbergasted. Not sure why but I just never thought of it like that.

Of course, we could talk about "what can I sell for $1,000" till the cows come home, but that honestly doesn't matter. Once you "get" the concept, you can be unstoppable.

That little piece of advice has made me more money than I ever could have imagined.

I'll end this with the third piece of advice he gave me; this is the piece I'm still working on, but it's equally as impactful and has made my life so much easier...

I asked him about how he gets so much done.

He said, "Jeremy, the day I learned to point was the day my business went to the next level."

Meaning, when you realize you can pay other people to do most of the work, everything changes.

It's really tough to grow a business past the 7-figure mark all by yourself.

I was a one-man show for so long, and I made a TON just like that.

But adding other people into the mix makes all the difference in the world and will allow you to grow to any level you desire.

As you can see from my story, I'm big on SIMPLICITY.

By nature, we all want to overcomplicate everything we do because society makes it feel like we are supposed to.

If this past decade has taught me anything it's that "boring works and simplicity rules."

If you feel like you're in a whirlwind of directions, take a step back and a deep breath.

Look at the core fundamentals, kill off everything else and focus more on that.

I've paid more money than I'd like to admit for "coaching and mentorship," and I've found that the absolute best mentors speak and teach with the most simplicity.

Matt is absolutely one of those people.

Just one of those guys who can speak a single sentence and change your entire existence.

I hope what I've shared impacts you, even in a tiny way.

Meet The Author:

Jeremy Kennedy is a 40-year-old entrepreneur from Arkansas. A single father of two boys, he's spent the last decade helping tens of thousands other people grow their businesses using the internet. His mission has been to help ordinary people make extraordinary income online. Jeremy also dedicated his life to helping people find truth as a Christian, sharing not only business but also the Bible. You're invited to find out more about Jeremy and how he can help you at

https://jeremykennedy.net

Just Show Up!

By Jeanne Kolenda

I'm almost 72 years old as I write this. I've had an amazing life, full of things both unexpected and planned. I've been dirt poor, and I can remember collecting soda bottles and cashing them in to get enough small change to buy baby food. I can remember always taking a small calculator to the grocery store to make sure I didn't put too many items in the cart because I had less than $50 in my checking account. But that was 50 years ago.

In the midst of all that, I raised two fantastic kids who are now my favorite people on the planet and my best friends. We tell those stories now and marvel at how things changed.

So how did I turn this around?

For one thing, I was motivated not just by money but by a desire to achieve freedom and flexibility; I wanted to live on my terms and never punch a clock. I've made that happen.

So, back to the title of this chapter – JUST SHOW UP!

For starters, I showed up one day back in 1989 when I was working as a consultant at a local computer store. I had become quite the local celebrity by publishing a small newspaper and featuring interviews with people whom I found fascinating. I loved telling stories.

The Apple Macintosh had just come out, and I was really good at making that small 9-inch screen come to life; it was the basis for my fledgling publishing venture. A local computer store had asked me to help sell this new-fangled thing to consumers, so I would show up and do small classes, and when they bought, I'd make a small commission. Remember – my goal was to NOT punch a clock!

So, I showed up one day at the store, and at the close of my demonstration, a handsome man walked in and stood in the back of the room observing. He wasn't dressed like most of us. I lived on a small barrier island in Georgia, and we were very casual. This guy had on a tweed jacket, a shirt and tie, and I KNEW he couldn't be a "local." He wasn't. He was from the west coast and was there to install some point-of-sale software and computers. He was the owner of the software company and had decided to do the installation himself so he could play golf at one of our famous courses. BUT...UPS had lost one of the monitors, and he was at the store to rent a monitor until UPS could locate the one lost.

I was at the end of a very troubled 20-year marriage, and I wasn't looking for romance. But something magical happened. I've now been married to that handsome stranger for 32 years.

BECAUSE I SHOWED UP THAT DAY!

Fast forward to 2012. We had moved to Myrtle Beach, SC, and my husband had taught me enough about business to help me start an automated answering service, which was a new thing back then, and I had taken over the market and actually put a live operator service out of business.

One problem – I was bored with it. It ran SO well there wasn't much to do; customers came to me and there wasn't even much selling to do. So, I began paying attention to what was happening with the internet. Seems that there was a lot of "buzz" about local marketing, the rise of Google and websites and mobile marketing.

I wanted it! But where to start?

I was in a motorcycle club from our church, and on a ride one day, I started talking to another gal who was also interested in local marketing. We decided to team up and start a business helping local businesses with their marketing. She had been a Microsoft-certified trainer, and she, too, was BORED! We built our business in some very unconventional ways, including doing free webinars for the local Chambers of Commerce. Yes, they were free, but lots of business owners reached out for help. The training was nice, but they didn't want to do this work for themselves. BINGO!

One day, I saw an ad online advertising a local marketing summit being held in Las Vegas. The only problem was – it was NEXT WEEK! No time to plan. Or was there? I bet you can guess what I did!

I hopped on a plane and was in Vegas the next week. I didn't know a single soul there.

BUT I JUST SHOWED UP!

That event was life-changing in more ways than I can count. Yes, I learned a lot; but more importantly, I met some key players, and I wasn't shy. My old journalistic nature rose to the surface, and I made it a point to spend a lot of time getting to know these fascinating guys. I've said I should have written a book called, "Me and Five Guys in Vegas!"

Two guys, in particular, were extremely interested in this "Chamber of Commerce" thing we were doing. They wanted to teach this to others, and they helped us build a product and they launched us into the JV marketing world.

Over the next few years, I went on to generate millions of dollars by doing joint ventures with these guys, and a few others who were there. My new friends were gracious and patient, and we were all winners...including the folks who bought the course.

I won't name-drop, but I bet some of you know who these guys are.

Now that I had some financial flexibility, I showed up to other places... Masterminds, other conferences, both large and small, cruises...

In fact, you wouldn't be reading this right now had I not shown up to a conference in Atlanta and met Matt Bacak.

Isn't it amazing what can happen with you JUST SHOW UP?!!

I can't help but mention a couple more times I showed up.

I went on a marketer's cruise one year. We cruised to Aruba and Curacao; there was one long day in port, and we didn't have to be back on the ship until 11 pm. Most folks chose to participate in some kind of water sports – scuba diving, jet skiing. But my husband, Leon, and I chose to take a jeep ride into the mountains. After all, we live at a beach, and we can go jet skiing any time we want.

Two more couples chose the jeep ride.

Mike and Lexie Lantz were one of those couples. He happens to own Warrior Plus, and even though I had purchased products, I'd never thought about making my own and selling them. Mike convinced me that I should do that. I did. The rest is history. I'm SO glad I showed up for that jeep ride.

And I'll share ONE more beautiful thing that happened when I just showed up.

I was at a conference in Orlando. Again, not being shy, I was making new friends and loving it. I thought I recognized one guy as someone I had purchased a product from. I was right. He, however, was a bit shy, but I didn't leave him any choice but to talk to me. LOL

He called me when we got home from the conference and asked if he could interview me on one of his coaching calls. Of course, I said yes. During that live coaching call, he asked me to come to Spain and speak at a Mastermind. I wanted to...but I needed to check with Leon and truth be told, I didn't want to go without him; he had to be ok with this. The man who offered this sensed my hesitation and promptly said, "Of course, I'll pay for you AND your husband to come!" Remember, this was on a live call...how could I say no?

OK...done deal! And Leon was thrilled.

So, we went...and while I was "working" Leon rented a motorcycle and rode all over the coast of Spain. We stayed an extra week and had one of the most memorable trips of our lives. I had to teach Leon how to use Google Translate on his phone, as he didn't speak a word of Spanish, but he did fine!

Think about what we would have missed if I hadn't SHOWN UP in Orlando and met this guy!

In closing, I got a little weary with SEO and all the Google dances, and I gave that up. In fact, I gave all the customers to my first partner (the one I was in the motorcycle club with). She loves that side of local marketing, and she's built it into a great business for herself and her hubby. We still have lunch often and our friendship is priceless.

I went on to build a social posting business, and I couldn't be more pleased. I love my B2B clients, and I'm still making courses and selling coaching and tools to other local agencies.

Oh...and remember one of those five guys in Vegas that helped me launch my first product? We're still close friends and working right now on something amazing together.

ALL BECAUSE I SHOWED UP!

So, before you turn down opportunities to show up, think about my story.

PS... We gave up the motorcycles a few years ago, bought an RV, and Leon and I and our two Standard Poodles, April and Andy, are still traveling and SHOWING UP... wherever we want! Next stop... to see grandsons (and their parents) in Texas. As long as I have the internet, a laptop, and a spare... we're good to go!

Meet The Author:

Jeanne Kolenda is married to Leon, is a mom to Edward and Melissa, a Bonus Mom to Noel, and grandmother to Jonathan (17), Drew (15) and Benjamin (11). She's lived in Myrtle Beach, SC for 32 years but she and Leon travel in their RV (along with their two Standard Poodles, April and Andy) several months a year. Edward and Melissa's spouses, Leigh-Ann and Randy, call her their "Mother-In-Love."

She's the oldest of 6 children, and there are now 60 people in the "tribe." (Siblings, spouses, children, grandchildren)

She's been a serial entrepreneur for 40 years and loves working from home (whether that's her house or her RV!) She and her husband, Leon, founded In Touch Solutions in 1994, a telecommunications company that services local businesses with tracking numbers and automated answering services.

She got into local internet marketing in 2012 and founded the Business Training Team with her friend, Sue White. Sue took that over in 2016 and Jeanne went on to focus on Social Media Posting. You can find her at https://localcontentdepot.com

She's also excelled at creating training courses for other Agency Owners and is a top 10% Vendor on Warrior Plus.

Her love of people, storytelling, and writing has resulted in her being featured in several books, this one being the second one with Matt Bacak.

She likes to say she's the Queen of "F" words!

Faith

Family

Friends

Freedom

Flexibility

And then there are her favorite "C" words:

Connect

Collaborate

Communicate

When asked what is something that would surprise people to know about her, she said this:

"I homeschooled my children before it was legal and was arrested for it one time. The charge was 'Contributing to the Delinquency of a Minor by way of Truancy." Those underprivileged children have gone on to get graduate degrees and speak several languages. HA!"

She likes to make up words for fun. Her two favorites:

Chaordic – Being chaotically organized

Refirement – Replaces retirement

You can find Jeanne here:

Facebook: Jeanne Beemer Kolenda

Email: jeannekolenda@gmail.com

Instagram: Jeanne.kolenda

Jeanne has been a Speaker and Instructor at conferences both on the topic of marketing and sometimes purely for inspiration. Feel free to reach out. Email is the best way.

https://shs.socialnichepacks.com/everyday-heroes-version-3-gift/?coupon=EDHV197

Something to be Proud Of

By Aaron Landreth

When I stumbled in the doors of Alcoholics Anonymous that Sunday morning at 8 a.m., I found my bottom.

The room opened before me, and a friendly stranger pointed to a seat.

He saw the shame on my face, when moments before, I apologized to my wife for having let her down...again.

She sped away in the car after she dropped me

off. My 1-year-old son was with her in his car

seat. She was frustrated and disappointed.

Deep down she didn't know if I was still the right one.

She gave me an ultimatum.

Stop lying.

Stop drinking.

Be the man I know you can be.

...Or we're done.

Timidly, I sat down on the cold metal chair.

I could smell the alcohol from the previous days on myself.

Nervousness and anxiety were already setting in.

Shakes, sweats, and agitation were on the way.

I hated withdrawals.

Too many times.

Too many failed attempts.

It's one of the reasons I continued to drink.

I drank no longer to seek pleasure.

It was to avoid pain...avoid withdrawal...and avoid fear.

It's tough to explain looking back.

Even harder to explain to a person who controls their drinking or doesn't drink at all.

The perceived fear that alcohol gives to a chronic drinker whose physiology has changed is all-consuming.

It's not perceived fear.

It's real.

As real as the trembling hands, sweaty forehead, and insomnia.

It's a fear that thwarts so many good intentions to stop.

In spite of the fear, I was already experiencing and soon to face,

this time I told myself it was "the last time."

But this was not one of those "this is the last time" you give yourself after a rough night.

This time I was determined…committed…all in.

My family was on the line.

I parked my fidgety body in the chair.

In my head, I repeated…

I will show my family I will be there for them.

I am a husband and a dad.

I have the power for a better future…for me and my family.

This is my last chance.

One by one, each of the men in the room began to share in front of the group.

One of the men's stories resonated with me deeply.

He shared how looking back on his life, he saw that he only gave half his effort.

In high school, he only did enough to graduate…though he knew he could do more.

When he graduated, he went to college…but only put in enough effort to pass.

When he got a job, he only worked enough to keep the bosses happy.

He saw that everywhere he looked in his life...

He only gave half his effort...only enough to get by.

His garage was a mess.

There were always dishes in the sink.

There were unfinished projects around the house...too many to count.

Drinking, for him, was a way to let all of this slide.

But he was tired of taking half-measures.

When he looked in the mirror - he was tired of feeling like he'd never grown up - tired of feeling like he'd never taken full responsibility.

And he realized in order to take control of his life and be the man he wanted to be...

...the man he knew he could be...

...he had to put drinking in the rearview mirror.

By the grace of God, he had done just that many years earlier and was living a fulfilled life.

When the other men in the room had all shared their stories, all eyes turned to me.

Normally, I would have sat and listened.

I wasn't one to share in front of a public group of strangers.

But this morning was different.

If I didn't take that step and asked for help, I was terrified I'd make the same poor choices I had in the past.

And this time the consequences were dire.

I shared how alcohol had turned me into a liar.

How my wife could no longer trust me.

How I hid my drinking from her and my family.

How ashamed I was for having made myself a liar.

How moments before, she dropped me off in the car and sped away with my son...

...and I wasn't sure if we'd still be together.

I shared how deathly afraid I was about the possibility of not being able to wake up in the same house as my son.

How I wouldn't be able to hold my son when he needed me.

I didn't blame her...How could she trust me?

I'd broken the trust in our marriage.

I didn't know if I could repair it.

I was broken, humiliated by my behavior.

But today, for the first time in a long time...I was honest.

When the meeting finished, the men in the room gathered around me and introduced themselves.

Although I wasn't proud of myself, they were proud of me.

They told me I was the most important man in the room that day.

I didn't get it then, but I get it now.

Most of them had been sober for years, some decades.

To see themselves in a man just starting his journey into sobriety strengthened their resolve.

Two of the men that day exchanged phone numbers with me.

They called that night and every night for weeks to check in on me.

They provided support and accountability.

They saw me through.

They helped save my marriage and my family.

It's many years later now, and I can't put into words how grateful and fortunate I am.

The men I met in the room that day are heroes.

They helped save me from me.

They helped alter the trajectory of my future and the future of my family.

I quit drinking.

I resolved to stop living only by half measures.

I resolved to live honestly...in my personal life and in business.

My wife stayed by my side.

I've been able to raise my son.

And what's more, our family grew, and I'm able to raise his little sister.

My heart swells as I type this and reflect.

There's so much to be thankful for

But without those men that day, none of this would be.

They are true heroes.

And I am forever grateful.

Meet The Author:

Aaron Landreth is a Husband, Father of 2, drug/alcohol rehab owner and a heart attack survivor at 38.

He is also the online coach and course creator who invented the F4ProfitAccelerator.com, a 3-step system that helps time strapped entrepreneurs make money online so they can confidently ditch their day job and gain more family time.

His mission is to empower 1,000 online entrepreneurs with the tools and strategies needed to shortcut their way to success so they can be there for their family when they need it most.

To access his unique 3-step system to build a profitable online business, he's inviting readers of Everyday Heroes to receive a very special free gift. Visit to claim your free gift: https://aaronlandreth.com/free-gift

Get Up, Get Up, Get Up!

by Alicia Lyttle

August 17th, 2010, I walked out on my husband, and Les Brown made me do it.

Les called me early one morning after hearing the disturbing news that I was battling cancer again. I was first diagnosed with ovarian cancer one year after marriage and quickly underwent surgery and treatments. Unfortunately, 18 months later, it returned, and this cycle would repeat itself throughout my marriage. A mutual friend had told Les that I was battling it again for the 5th time. When I answered Les's phone call, he said, "Alicia, I know why this is happening to you, and there's something that I need you to do for me. The next time your husband walks toward you, I need you to tell me how your body feels on the inside." "On the inside?" I asked. "Yes, Alicia, on the inside," Les Brown said.

Les then began to teach me about a term he coined 'relationship illness,' and he asked me if I'd ever heard the statement: 'that person makes me sick.' I uttered, "Yes, I have heard that term before; what are you trying to get at?" "Well, it's true. People really can make you physically sick. Your relationship, how he treats you, and the stress he puts you in is the root cause of your cancer. You are in a toxic relationship." I need you to tell me how your body feels the next time you see him walking towards you and call me back," he said, and then abruptly hung up the phone.

Shortly after, I saw my husband parading towards my office as I peeped out the back window towards the pool house he converted into his office and studio. He was so unpredictable that I wasn't sure if he would yell at me for something, laugh and tell a joke, or rattle off instructions for me to do something for him. Following Les's instructions, I connected with my inner self, closed my eyes, and shockingly witnessed that my body was boiling on the inside. How could I have not noticed this before?

Once he arrived in my office, he spewed off a few complaints about his breakfast not being hot enough. Then, he interrogated me on when I would be delivering lunch to his office. Then reminded me to check his emails for him and not to disturb him while he was playing his video games.

My ex-husband had an obscenely loud alarm on his phone that went off two times a day at 12 noon and 7 pm, and if his meals were not delivered at those exact times, pandemonium would break loose in the house. I hired a woman to help me cook his meals and take them to him on time, but unfortunately, she was out that day.

97

As soon as he left my office, I called Les Brown and said to Les, "I was boiling on the inside!" Les said calmly, "Get out as quickly as you can. if you want to live, you must muster up the courage to leave."

The business was a super successful multi-million-dollar company; we lived in a huge mansion, drove luxury cars, and only traveled first class. Although I had thought about leaving dozens of times, I had spent the last ten years of my life building a business with him, and I feared the repercussions that might fall on our staff and our clients if I left.

The opportunity to leave would come soon enough. A few weeks later, I got a call from my husband's assistant saying she found out he was going on a trip with another woman. I asked her not to say anything, and I used this as my opportunity to get out.

While he was on vacation with his mistress, I packed up, took my suitcase, laptop, and cell phone, and drove away. Once he returned home and noticed I was gone, he threatened me, saying if I didn't return, he'd make my life a living hell. He worked hard to deliver on that promise and locked me out of our business, the bank accounts, credit cards, and the house, and kept me from ever seeing any of my five dogs ever again. My sister and mother also worked in the business, and he locked them out of everything because I left. I was 34 years old and at one of the lowest points in my life.

I ended up sleeping on my sister's sofa, down on myself for the situation I was now facing. One day while lying on that sofa wallowing in self-pity, my phone rang, and it was Les Brown. "Alicia, what are you doing?"

"Les, I'm lying on the sofa." Then I started my pity party by telling him how I worked every day in the business and was left with nothing; he would not even give me one of the five dogs we had and how this was so unfair.

As one might expect, Les stopped me mid-conversation and said, "Alicia, you've landed on your back, but you can look up, so GET UP" then he said GET UP, and his voice got louder, and he repeated it, GET UP, and then in that deep Les Brown power voice he said GEEEETTTTT UUUUUPPPPPP! You have Greatness within you; tap into it right now!" and he once again abruptly hung up the phone!

I jumped off the sofa, went to my sister's room, and said, " You know what, we're going to start over. We must have something of value that someone else would be willing to pay us for." And at that moment, my sister and I launched our new business, which has gone on to make millions of dollars.

When faced with something that seems like destruction, you can become bitter and sour and let that poison the rest of your life.

It's not easy but keep moving forward. You might have to dig down deep. Know that there are good days ahead, and you get to choose how to live your life every day. Are you going to stay on the sofa or GET UP?

Today, my core business is teaching people how to tap into that greatness within, pull out their skills and talents, and turn them into an online business. I teach people that no matter what situation they are in right now, they have the opportunity to change it by pulling out the greatness within them.

That day, I was forced to get up, so I started a side hustle that became so successful that I started teaching others how to start a side hustle online. I conduct free workshops on my website www.freelancinggenius.com that have changed so many lives it brings me pure joy! My sister and I have been blessed to have traveled all over the world, from Nigeria and South Africa to Australia, New Zealand, Singapore, Malaysia, the United Kingdom all over the Caribbean, and the United States, teaching others to leverage the power of the internet to create financial freedom.

What do you have within you that you can turn into an online business and transform your future? Let's walk through three steps to get you on the right path. The first step is to identify what skills and talents you already have that others would be willing to pay you for. Most people go through life without really tapping into their skills and talents. One of my favorite authors, Erma Bombeck, said, "When I stand before God at the end of my life, I would hope that I would not have a single bit of talent left, and could say, 'I used everything you gave me." Are you using everything you have?

The next step is to identify what skills you've always wanted to learn that people would be willing to pay you for. Every skill you acquire increases your ability to level up. Today we have YouTube and Google, and the knowledge is out there when we search for those things we want to learn. Have a deep hunger for acquiring new talents and skills that if you don't fill up daily with the knowledge, you feel the emptiness in your stomach as you starve for more.

The last step is putting yourself on social media and sites like fiverr.com, upwork.com, and freelancer.com. Self-promotion has never been easier than today in the era of Social Media. You have to get out there and give it everything you've got! Push yourself. There will never be a better time to start, so push yourself; the world is waiting for you.

So, what are you going to do with that greatness you have? Whatever your greatness is, what are you going to do with it?

We all have seeds of greatness, skills, and talents that others would be willing to pay us for.   Nelson Mandela said, "There is no passion to be found playing small

— in settling for a life that is less than the one you are capable of living." Today you are in the position to make a living around what you are passionate about, so have the courage to live a life that is true to yourself.

Yes, I'm cancer free and in a fantastic relationship, and my new business with my sister has far surpassed the old business. The one thing I want to leave you with is that when you need to talk yourself into your greatness, remember these words by Les Brown, Get up, Get up, GET UP!

If there is anything that you feel I could do to help you on your journey, I invite you to reach out to me on Social Media, on my website www.alicialyttle.com, or check out my workshop at www.freelancinggenius.com.

Meet The Author:

Business owner, Business Coach, International Speaker & Trainer.

Before jumping into entrepreneurship, Alicia was enrolled in the Ph.D. program at the University of Michigan, pursuing a career in Environmental Science and Policy. She worked with notable organizations, including The White House, The United States Environmental Protection Agency (USEPA), and The City of New Orleans in the Mayor's Office.

In 2000, she was introduced to how to build a business via the Internet and left her Ph.D. behind. In 2010 she experienced several setbacks, from battling cancer and walking away from a marriage that left her from being a millionaire to being flat-broke. She bounced back, and with hard work and dedication, today, she is a self-made millionaire through her online ventures.

As a well-sought-after speaker and trainer, Alicia has traveled the world to places such as Singapore, China, Australia, the United Kingdom, New Zealand, South Africa, and throughout the United States. Not only does she speak on stage, but she is a regular guest on podcasts, radio shows, local news stations, and more, all emphasizing how to leverage the Internet to work from anywhere, be your own boss and build the lifestyle you deserve and desire.

Alicia is the founder of Pow Social, a Digital Marketing Agency based on the island of Jamaica with clients such as the National Commercial Bank and Hertz. She also produces a weekly segment on Jamaica's public broadcasting channel (PBCJ) called The Digital JamPrenuer that teaches everyday people how to use the internet to improve their lives.

Alicia's goal is to help others recognize their brilliance and turn that brilliance into profits by leveraging the power of the Internet. Alicia believes that the internet is the great equalizer allowing people from all backgrounds to build wealth regardless of their past.

Social Media Links:

Facebook: https://www.facebook.com/aliciarosettalyttle
Facebook Business: https://www.facebook.com/alicialyttlejamaica
Instagram: https://www.instagram.com/alicialyttle/
LinkedIn: https://www.linkedin.com/in/alicialyttle/
YouTube: https://youtube.com/alicialyttle
Pinterest: www.pinterest.com/alicialyttle
Clubhouse: https://www.clubhouse.com/@alicialyttle
Website: www.alicialyttle.com

Being Unstoppable

by Ricky Mataka

I'm just a normal guy... had a rough childhood and upbringing, so I was not your posterboard kind of kid, to say the least... but one thing I did was do first and ask questions later. I got into programming in 2003 and decided that I was going to make my money selling products online, but I was completely clueless about what value I bring to the world... plus I was broke and could not afford to have people build my sites, so I learned to do it myself.

Through my struggles of trying to make money online, I came up short of a lot of my expectations. It was through countless hours, hard work, and consistency that I was able to get some results ...

I took a risk in 2007 - spent my rent money and went to an event that I thought would change my life... and I'm glad I did... I landed a job with a high-profile marketer that showed me the ins and outs of a 25-million-dollar online operation. I absorbed it like a sponge as I fell asleep on my keyboard countless times, programming for the company.

In 2011, I took the risk to do this for myself, and I never looked back since... I have grossed over 40 million in my career and helped thousands of people live the life they deserve.

It's through risk and strong willpower that I tackled the obstacles thrown at me and took my many failures as successful dreaming...

When I started out, having absolutely no clue what I was doing, I was developing an excellent SEO software opportunity but had zero skills with sales and webinars. I was given the chance to perform my first webinar in front of 1000 people. It was do or die in 2011. Either I made it work or it was back to programming. So, it was just me reading a script from an iPad. All very low-tech, but I ended up closing 40k that night. Needless to say, I learned a lot of lessons, but by the end of that year, my business partners and I closed just under $1M in sales.

Since then, I've worked as a consultant to help other people launch sales webinar systems. Many of those have gone on to do 6 or even 7-figure launches.

I'm not just about trying to sell pretty software. I want to help people succeed.

I have dedicated countless hours to the success of many companies as well as my own products. I've stayed up all night, doing whatever it takes to achieve the success I have today. I've made a major impact on people's lives and revenue, and that's what has made me the sort of marketer I am today. So, your takeaway from reading this should be to believe in your worth and value, do whatever is necessary, and take what works from wherever you can find it. Cause once you find it, it'll be hard to stop you!

You can learn more about me @ rickymataka.com

Meet The Author:

Ricky Mataka is a serial entrepreneur, 20+ year Ninja Coder & 7 Figure Earner. Ricky is known for his multi six-figure presentation experience and software platforms that change the lives of many of his students. Having spoken on stage across multiple high-profile events, he has built up an array of resources and inspiration across the industry.

Ricky also runs a high scale group of over 10,000+ members that look up to Ricky as being a mentor, friend and action taker that provides proven Stats.

You can learn more about me @ rickymataka.com

What Makes a Father

by Zach Maxwell

There are pros and cons to growing up without a father in the house. On one hand, growing up without a father can provide a chance to learn how to be independent and self-sufficient; it can teach you how to look to other positive males in your life for guidance and reassurance. However, it can be very challenging to watch other children with their father and tough not having a male role model around.

My own experience growing up without a father was a mix of both pros and cons. I always wondered who my father was, what he was doing in life, and where he might be. However, I have been fortunate that my grandfather and uncle filled the "father" role for me, so I never had to wonder what having a father was like. Another positive is that I learned how to be independent and self-sufficient at an early age, and in some ways, I think that made me a stronger person.

Of course, every situation is different. Some kids growing up without a father-figure end up feeling angry or resentful; perspective is an amazing thing. Others find alternate role models to look up to and fill the void in their life. Either way, I think it's safe to say that growing up without a father can be tough. It's important to have someone to talk to about these feelings if you're going through them, and it's also important to remember you're not alone. There are plenty of other people in the world who have gone through the same thing.

Growing up without a father in the house, I never felt I was missing out. I didn't need a father. My uncle Michael and grandfather Doug Maxwell filled that role naturally and taught me everything I would have learned from a father, and more. They taught me how to be a man, how to work hard, and how to treat women with respect. They showed me what it means to be a family man and how to be there for my loved ones. They instilled in me the importance of education and hard work. I am grateful to them for their guidance and support. Without them and all the lessons that they taught me, I wouldn't be the man I am today.

My uncle Michael was always there for me when I needed someone to talk to, and he was always happy to offer advice and guidance. My grandfather Doug was also a great role model, and he taught me a lot about hard work and determination. Without their support, I don't know where I would be. They both helped shape me throughout my most formative years, and I am grateful for everything they did for me.

When I was preparing to write this, I asked my aunt to help me get information from my father figures in their own words, so that I could see from their perspective what being a father really means to them. They are not only two of the smartest, happiest men I know, but they are also the best father figures a boy could hope for.

My Uncle Michael wrote, "I believe that being a good father requires you to be present in the home. You must lead by example in how you act with your wife, treating her as your equal. You must be patient with your children and give guidance in situations they may not understand. It is important to be the parent and not the friend.

Never be afraid to admit when you're wrong or made a mistake as a parent. Your children will respect you far more if they know you are not afraid to say, "I'm sorry." This does not mean to apologize for everything they get mad at you about. What I'm talking about is instances where you, as a parent, make a comment or a decision that later, when you reflect and think to yourself, "That was not the right way or place to make that comment, especially in front of my child." In this instance, you should apologize for your misstep. This is an example of bringing your mistake out into the open and discussing it, talk about why you were wrong, and apologize.

Every child is a gift. Our nephew, Zachary, was the first gift I was granted. I have been able to be involved in his life since day one, loving him, encouraging him, praying for him, doting on him, cherishing him, and being so proud of him. I would happily claim him any day and I give thanks to God every day that I have been able to be so involved in his life.

In mine and my wife's circumstance, we fought for all four of our children, whether it was getting pregnant, staying pregnant, or going through the adoption process with two of our children. They were each a blessing that required faith, prayer, and steadfast determination to get them here. I would also say that those three things are only the beginning, and you must keep going when your children are growing and finding their own way.

I was 27 years old when we had our first biological child, Ella. I remember the first time I held her alone. It was when my wife took her first shower after having Ella, so I beat my chest like I was the king and held my child without any fear… until the bathroom door closed, and I was alone with her for the first time. I had what I believe is a panic attack. This person is my responsibility. I must make sure she's fed, clothed, taken care of, loved to no end. I freaked out, but it only lasted for a brief second. Then I was overcome with joy and ready to step up to the call.

It prepared me for what was to come. We were challenged again to stay pregnant with Rubye, and not a single worry of how I was going to be a father, now to two children ever crossed my mind. When our boys moved in just two months before Rubye was born, the same held true. I was excited and ready. I had faith that God was at work and every special way our children came into our lives was by design. That is so comforting.

Any male can "father" a child. It is maturity and selflessness that is required to be a father in the true sense of the word. This basic rule doesn't change, even with our society that is consistently making it easier for the father to be absent. The single most important thing for the family is to live your life with Christian values and to be that example for your children. Love them unconditionally. It won't be without challenges, but nothing of any value comes easily."

I'm sure that after reading his perspective, you already have an idea of what a phenomenal man he is, but for you to fully comprehend the impact he had on my life, I want to tell you a little about growing up with him involved in my life every single day. I grew up living next door to my Aunt Sissy and Uncle Michael. When I was little, I would go to their house every day because it was one of my favorite places to be. They always treated me like a son, and we had so much fun together. Their home has always been one of love, faith, fairness, respect, empathy, safety, creativity, and kindness.

My uncle is the one who taught me how to play sports, my favorite being baseball. When I was very young, his work had a softball team, and he would take me to all their games; he even got me my own team tee shirt and told me I was their good luck mascot. I loved every minute of it. As I grew older and became involved in recreational baseball, he would always coach me and encourage me to be the best player I could possibly be by working hard to develop my talents. It is because of him that I went on to play in the Latin American World Series for two years in a row. He never let me give up and because of that I went on to live, dream, and gain experiences that not only made me a better player but also made an impact that I will never forget.

Uncle Michael is also the reason I discovered sales. He is a sales manager for the company he works for and puts his all into being an amazing representative for his company and their product. He is dedicated and works hard. He does this not only to provide for his family, but also because he believes a good work ethic is important and helps show one's character.

I consider my uncle Michael a blessing, not just to me, but to everyone he comes into contact with. He truly is one of the best, and I want to be just like him. My goals came from his teaching, leadership, and example, and that is something that I will always be thankful for. I hope that one day I can repay him for everything he has done and given me.

But my blessings don't stop there. My grandfather was the other instrumental man in my life. He too helped mold me into a productive member of society. He has always been involved in my life and has always reminded me of my worth. Here are his thoughts on being a father.

"Being a father can be the most difficult thing a man ever does, or it can be the easiest. It can be the most rewarding thing, or the most thankless. It can bring pride or disappointment, pain or pleasure, strength or weakness. It is a roller-coaster of experiences from one end of the spectrum to the other. But, of all my life experiences, it has been one of the most fulfilling and enjoyable opportunities I have ever been given.

My wife, Laura, and I were married young. I was 21 and she was 20. We waited 5 years before we had our first daughter, Jennifer, and then another 5 years for our daughter, Stephanie's, birth. They were two of the most beautiful things I had ever seen. We both loved them, nurtured them, and tried to always make them feel safe. Looking back, my life was so busy with work, going to college at night, and building a house that more of the parenting fell on my wife than it should have. I tried to always set a good example, though not always with the best outcome.

My children always knew we were there to support them and to lean on when they needed us.

Raising girls is probably easier than raising boys. Discipline, swift but just, is key in developing good, happy children. Girls don't seem to be quite as mischievous as boys, and consequently, discipline was much easier in our home than most.

Our girls were brought up to know of the one true God and His love for them. Church involvement was always part of their lives and is probably a major reason they are good, honest adults today.

Teaching work ethic is something that needs to start at a young age. Too many children have no responsibilities or tasks, and that leads to laziness in adult life.

You should be respectful to children, as you would to an adult if you ever expect them to respect you. Screaming at your children is as successful as screaming at adults.

Treat them fairly, love them, discipline them, listen to them, and make time for them. They must know that you love them as God loves them. But don't spoil them!"

Growing up, I lived in my grandfather and grandmother's house. This allowed me to have many more experiences with my grandparents than most other kids have. My grandfather and I did everything together, had countless adventures, and we were always up to something. He taught me how important it is to use my mind to solve problems, not just my muscles. From him I learned how to fix cars and airplanes; he'd teach me patiently and comprehensively anything I wanted to know. He taught me complex things that many people go to school to learn, and he believed in my ability to learn so much that he started teaching me these things at a very early age. We have a bond with each other that no one can sever; to this day I still consider him to be my best friend. It is hard to adequately describe just how amazing he is and what a profound impact he has had on my life. He showed me the importance of family and how the ones you love should always come first. If I could wish for anything, it would be to spend more time with him.

There are many people who think that life is so much harder when growing up without a father, but for me the truth is that not having a father in my life didn't matter. What really matters in this situation is whether or not there are courageous, loving, devoted men to fill that void and take on the role themselves. In my circumstance, I was fortunate enough to have two father figures who whole-heartedly took on the role of being my "father" and who showed me more love, and continue to show me more love, than some people are granted in a lifetime. What we need more of are people who are excited about impacting someone's life in a positive way and changing their future for the better; to me, these people are the true everyday heroes.

Meet The Author:

My Name is Zachary Maxwell. I am 19 years old. I grew up in a small town in Georgia called Brooks. I worked fast food, plumbing, electrical, construction, almost everything you can think of. But I shortly found my niche working with Matt Bacak and it is the best thing I have ever done. I moved out at 18 and have been making it on my own. I played baseball for team USA but didn't follow that path. I decided to get into Digital Marketing interning under Matt Bacak. It was the best decision I have ever made, and I am so thankful for the chance to learn. I dedicated this chapter to my grandfather and my uncles because I am here today because of them.

112

The Missing Link to Making Money Online

by Anthony McCarthy

What is the missing link to making money online? What is the piece that every single person is missing?

What would you say if I told you that having more money isn't so much about changing the way you work as much as it is changing the way you think? And what if I told you that you have the ability to make as much money as you want?

Would you say I was crazy? Off my rocker? Not making any sense?

I certainly understand that. After all, for our entire lives, we've been told that the only way to have more money is to either:

- Win the lottery

- Work harder

The odds of you winning the lottery are small – and besides, there's a much better way to make money.

And while there's certainly some truth that you must work hard if you want money, you can have as much money as you want without necessarily working harder.

Yes, for real!

See, here's the thing…

There's not a direct correlation between how hard you work and how much money you make.

Especially if you work for a salary. After all, you can work incredibly hard and only get a 3% raise every year.

No matter how hard you work…

…you're still going to be limited by your salary.

However, there is a direct correlation between your money mindset and how much money you make.

In other words, the way you think about money has a real and direct influence on how much money you actually make.

Your money mindset can either:

- Catapult you to wealth

- Keep you in poverty

That's how powerful it is.

This is why most people never reach the level of success they truly want. They don't have an effective mindset about achieving success and gaining wealth. They're trapped where they are and don't know how to change.

They've done things a certain way for so long that they can't see any other way of doing them.

In his book Secrets Of The Millionaire Mind, T. Harv Ecker says:

The reality is that most people do not reach their full potential. Most people are not successful. Research shows that 80 percent of individuals will never be financially free in the way they'd like to be, and 80 percent will never claim to be truly happy. The reason is simple. Most people are unconscious. They are a little asleep at the wheel. They work and think on a superficial level of life—based only on what they can see. They live strictly in the visible world.

Does this describe you?

- Not reaching your full potential?

- Not financially free?

- Not truly happy?

- Asleep at the wheel?

You know that you should be achieving great things...

...but you just can't quite seem to get there.

Then this is for you.

This will teach you how to change your mind and truly change your life. It will blow up many of the myths that you've believed for years and help reshape your thinking.

The only prerequisite for reading this book is an open mind.

Some of what you're about to read may contradict beliefs you've held about yourself and money for years. These beliefs have been holding you back from reaching your true potential.

It's time for those beliefs to be put to rest and for you to embrace the true reality of who you are.

It's time to stop being unconscious - asleep at the wheel - and to wake up to your greatness.

Ready?

Let's get started.

There's a good chance that what you believe about money is simply wrong. We've been conditioned by society, by our parents, and by our friends to believe certain things about money.

And most of us have believed those things without EVER questioning them.

Again, to quote T. Harv Ecker:

You were taught how to think and act when it comes to money. These teachings become your conditioning, which becomes automatic responses that run you for the rest of your life. Unless, of course, you intercede and revise your mind's money files.

As a result, we have what you might call a "difficult" relationship with money:

- We want more of it but can't ever seem to get enough.

- We know that money can achieve good things, but we feel conflicted when we spend it.

- We're grateful when we have the money to purchase the things we want, but also feel like we're being selfish.

Why do we have this relationship with money? Why do we get so tied up in knots over it? Why do we stress about it so much?

It's because we've believed a lot of myths and lies about money.

And we've never questioned our beliefs to see if they're actually true. And because we've never questioned them, we haven't achieved the level of success that we truly want.

In her book You Are A Badass At Making Money, Jen Sincero says:

Our beliefs, along with our thoughts and words, are at the root of everything we experience in life, which is why consciously choosing what rolls around in your mind and falls out of your mouth is one of the most important things you can do. This conscious choosing of your thoughts, beliefs, and words is called mastering your mindset, and master it you must if you'd like to live large and in charge.

If you want more success, money, and happiness, then it's crucial that you stop believing money myths and master your mindset about money.

Mastering your money mindset requires dispelling the myths you've believed for so long.

Let's look at some of the common myths we've believed about money.

MONEY MYTH #1: MONEY IS EVIL

We've all heard it said that money is the root of all evil. Maybe your parents reinforced this myth when you were growing up. They didn't want to accumulate too much money because they were afraid that it would result in evil.

And so, you've unconsciously adopted this belief.

- You don't want to accumulate too much money because you're afraid of what it

115

will do to you.

- You believe that somehow money will turn you evil.

- Or you believe that money itself is evil.

But is this true? Is money actually evil?

No.

Take a minute and think about what money actually is.

Money is simply printed paper. Or a chunk of metal, like a gold bar. Or just digital numbers in your bank account that go up and down.

Is that paper or metal inherently evil?

Nope.

Money itself is neutral. It's not good and it's not bad.

Think about it this way. When you put a $20 bill in your wallet, does that make you a worse person?

Of course not.

What if you put a $100 bill in your wallet?

You're still not a bad person.

That's because money itself is not evil. It's morally neutral.

Adding more money to your bank account doesn't mean that you're somehow adding something bad to your life. You're simply adding more numbers to your account.

Here's the key point: It's what you do with money, not money itself, that is good and bad.

- You can do great good with money.

- You can give it to people in need.

- You can buy something for yourself that you really want.

- You can start a charity.

- You can help your friend start a business.

And, of course, you can also do bad things with money.

You get the point. It's the actions you take, not money itself, that is evil.

So let's put this myth to bed. Money is neutral, not evil.

MYTH #2: PEOPLE WHO WANT MONEY ARE GREEDY

Many of us carry around the assumption that only people who are greedy want more money. We assume that if we want money, we'll become like Ebenezer Scrooge, always hoarding money but never giving it away.

116

But is this true?

No.

Again, money is a neutral thing. It's what you do with money that truly matters.

So yes, you can be greedy and simply want to accumulate as much money as possible.

But having more money also allows you to be extremely generous. It allows you to give good things to others. It allows you to donate to charity.

You simply can't do those things if you don't have money.

Did you catch that?

You can't be generous if you don't have money.

Think about that for a minute.

If you want to be financially generous, you have to have some finances in the first place.

It's time to kill this myth. Wanting more money does not make you greedy.

MYTH #3: THERE IS NOT ENOUGH MONEY

If you grew up in a house where finances were regularly "tight", then you may harbor the belief that there is not enough money.

You believe that the reason you don't have enough money is because there simply isn't enough money to go around.

But let's step back a minute and evaluate this belief.

How much money is in the world?

Trillions and trillions of dollars.

There is more than enough money for everyone. There is not a scarcity of money.

In fact, there is an actual abundance of money in the world.

Just because you don't have all the money that you want doesn't mean that there's not enough money.

This is the difference between a "scarcity" mindset and an "abundance" mindset:

- With a scarcity mindset, you believe that there is never enough. You feel like you have to hold onto everything you have because you never know when it will be gone.

- With an abundance mindset, you believe that there is more than enough for everyone. When you get money, it doesn't mean that someone else is not getting money.

So, as you see, money is not a zero-sum game. In other words, you receiving money does not mean that someone else is losing money.

That's not how it works.

There is more than enough money in the world for everyone to have as much as they want.

Let's kill this myth. There's plenty for everyone. We live in a world of abundance.

MYTH #4: I'LL NEVER MAKE ENOUGH MONEY

If you believe that you'll never make enough money, then you certainly will never make enough money.

But why do you have that belief in the first place?

If there is more than enough money in the world for everyone, why should you believe that you'll never make enough?

You're an incredibly talented person that has so much to offer the world, and it's critical that you believe that. Your skills, talents, and expertise are worth money, and there are lots of people out there who are willing to pay for those skills.

But in order for this to be your reality, you have to believe it first.

You have to stop buying into the lie that you'll never make enough money and start affirming that you are going to make more than you could imagine.

You may not know exactly how you're going to make the money, but that's okay.

You have to master your mindset, and that means having the unshakeable belief that you're going to increase your income.

Let's kick this myth to the curb. You can and will make more than enough money if you're willing to believe it first.

MYTH #5: IF I MAKE MORE MONEY, PEOPLE WON'T LIKE ME

This is a common myth that many people believe, especially if their parents didn't like people who had money.

But the reality is we don't dislike people who make money. We dislike people who flaunt their wealth in an arrogant way.

Again, this goes back to how you use

your money.

If you make more money and then start bragging to your friends about how awesome you are, then sure, they might not like you anymore.

But if you use your increased income to help others, people will actually like you more! And they certainly won't begrudge you for spending some on yourself.

This myth needs to go far away. As long as you don't flaunt your wealth in an annoying, arrogant way, you'll be just fine. In fact, people will probably appreciate you more as you accumulate wealth.

MYTH #6: I'M JUST FINE WITHOUT MONEY

If you've struggled for a long time to achieve financial stability, then you may have

118

convinced yourself that you're just fine without having any money.

But is this really true?

- Are you really living your absolute best life?

- Are you the best version of yourself that you can be?

- Are you able to live fearlessly, generously, and joyfully?

Let's be honest: money makes many things possible that aren't possible otherwise.

Money allows you to expand your horizons by traveling the world. It allows you to deepen friendships by going out to dinner with your close friends. It allows you to support worthy causes.

If you don't have money, you can't expand into your full potential. You can't be your best self.

To be clear, I'm not saying that people without money are somehow defective. That's wrong thinking. I'm simply saying that money gives you options that you wouldn't have otherwise.

Let's be done with this myth. It's time for you to achieve your true greatness.

Your mind is an incredibly powerful thing. Far more powerful than you can even imagine.

What you think about has an incredible effect on the quality of your life and whether you reach your dreams. In fact, your brain controls most of your reality:

- What you think about...

- What you give your attention to...

- What you focus on...

...literally controls the outcomes in your life.

Marcus Aurelius said:
The happiness of your life depends upon the quality of your thoughts. Therefore, guard accordingly, and take care that you entertain no notions unsuitable to virtue and reasonable nature.

This is true. The happiness of your life and the reality you create depends primarily upon your thoughts. That's how powerful your brain is.

If you want to be happy and attract wealth, it's crucial to adopt a certain mindset.

You must have a mindset of abundance.

Because of this, it's absolutely essential that we learn to master the way we think about wealth and abundance.

What most people fail to realize is that their mind creates almost all of the outcomes in their lives. Every outcome you're experiencing right now, whether it's positive or

119

negative, is primarily the result of your thoughts.

Or, to put it another way, what you constantly think about shapes your reality.

Your focus determines what you attract:

- Focus on positive things and you'll attract positive things.

- Focus on negative things and you'll attract the negative.

Yes, your mind really is that powerful.

Again, as Jen Sincero says:
...we can literally create the reality we desire by making ourselves think and believe what we desire to think and believe. How awesome is that?!

Or as T. Harv Ecker puts it:
Whatever results you're getting, be they rich or poor, good or bad, positive or negative, always remember that your outer world is simply a reflection of your inner world. If things aren't going well in your outer life, it's because things aren't going well in your inner life. It's that simple.

Are you starting to get the picture? As Ecker says, your outer world (reality) is simply a reflection of your inner world (your thoughts, desires, and dreams).

If you're not experiencing what you want in your life, it's primarily due to what's happening in your inner world.

- Not attracting the wealth you want? Inner world.

- Not able to get your head above water financially? Inner world.

- Not able to move forward in your job like you should? Inner world.

The good news is that you are the one in control of your inner world.

You determine what you think about and focus on. The more you control and shape your inner world, the more you will control and shape your actual reality.

Isn't that amazing to think about?

The massive implication is that if you want to change your life and attract more wealth, you absolutely must master the way you think.

If your outer world is a reflection of your inner world, then it's absolutely essential that you master your mindset about money. You need to be done with the myths from your past and adopt an abundance mindset.

If you have a scarcity mindset, believing that there is never enough money, then that is exactly what you will attract into your life. You will attract scarcity. You attract exactly what you focus on.

But if you believe in the abundance of the world, you'll attract abundance into your life. If you believe that there is more than enough for you and everyone else, you'll begin manifesting that in your life.

120

What you believe becomes your reality.

Therefore, it's important to believe:

- There's enough money for everyone.

- You simply need to reach out and take it.

Think about all the abundance in the world. You simply need to open yourself up to receive it.

Whether you believe in God or universal intelligence or the energy behind all things, you must believe that it wants you to have money. Because it really does.

The world is full of abundance, and if you're living in scarcity, then you're not enjoying all that the world has to offer.

It's time to change your mind about money. To believe that there's enough, that you deserve to have money, and that you were created to experience abundance.

Regularly affirm this. Tell yourself these things over and over again until they're burned into your brain. Until you believe them with all your heart and soul.

Once you start having an abundance mindset and open yourself up to all that the Creator wants to give you, you'll start seeing opportunities everywhere.

- You'll see ways to acquire money that you never would have seen before.

- Opportunities will drop into your lap out of nowhere.

- You'll begin to attract money in ways that surprise you.

But you must open your mind to the possibilities that are all around you. The world is full of infinite possibilities, and just because you can't see them doesn't mean they're not there.

Angelina Zimmerman puts it this way:

The scarcity pathway leads one to experience a life not fully lived, a life that can only be described as pedestrian. Overflowing with strong negative reactions like the high tide that creates waves in a rock pool not to mention the countless missed opportunities and experiences.

Those that choose to walk along the path of abundance experience a completely different life. Opting to live life to the full, exuding happiness, generous by nature, creative and inspirational. Taking full advantage and enjoying the wave of opportunities that come their way, along with memorable experiences.

Today, choose the path of abundance.

One of the best ways to choose abundance is through the practice of gratitude.

Start practicing gratitude for all the ways that the Creator has got your back and is bringing abundance into your life. When you receive something good and positive, say a simple, "Thank you." This practice will start to transform the way you live.

121

When you're grateful for even the smallest things, it puts positive energy out into the world, which then attracts more positive things into your life.

It really is a powerful cycle. You put out the positive energy of gratitude and you are rewarded with more things to be grateful for.

Amazing, isn't it?

So, begin practicing gratitude immediately. As you shift your mindset from scarcity to abundance, you'll be shocked by all the good things that start to come into your life.

There is an amazing future out there, just waiting for you to seize it. Don't let that future pass you by. Don't arrive 30 years from now and regret the actions that you didn't take.

Master your money mindset today and watch what begins to happen. You'll be absolutely floored by the results!

Meet The Author:

Anthony Mc Carthy is a 40-year sales and marketing veteran, who is now a full time Online Education Entrepreneur, with 3 decades of online and offline sales and marketing.

Over the past ten years Anthony has helped countless business owners use the internet and social media to digitize their business.

A strong track record in brand engagement, brand awareness and community for brands. By combining social media and mobile, he helps brands get in front of their market.

He is an international speaker on Marketing Online and using the web to automate and grow your business.

Anthony has had the honor of consulting for the Irish Government on a number of times, on use of social media, startups etc.

Attracting Permission, Your Key to Access, Power, & Wealth (How to Gain It Quickly and Almost Effortlessly)

by Barry C. McLawhorn

I grew up in an environment of absolute lack (at least financially), in the heart and soul of the rugged and self-reliant Appalachian Mountains. I was the son of a poor preacher. When I say absolute lack, in a "village" with a total population of 67 at the time, some still did not have running water and a few even still had outhouses or privies in their backyards. But the lack only made me more persistent and more determined to rise above my humble beginnings.

I took my first real job at age 7. I can remember it to this day. I interviewed with the president of the Ruritan National Headquarters (my father's good friend) in his big office, and he reached across his big desk and shook my hand as he congratulated me for getting the job as the new lawn care person for his organization.

Little did I realize that I had just followed a path that would be the cornerstone of my career and my life. More about that later, but first a bit more about that pivotal day in the life of a young man.

I came home and proudly told my father, who had introduced me to Mr. Mady, that I had gotten the job. The next day at Newbern Elementary School, I bragged to my classmates that I had gotten a job, and that I would be "going to work" after school that day. At the time I carried a "briefcase" to school - it was a Fisher Price red plastic pegboard carrying case with a blackboard on the other side. It was about two inches thick and held all of the priceless prize possessions of a budding entrepreneur. On any given day the contents could include a Trim pocketknife (purchased proudly from the Rest Areas on the deadly West Virginia Turnpike) with my chore and allowance money. Balls of string. Pencils. Pink Pearl erasers. An empty Bayer Aspirin tin, and a newly found bird feather, special rock, or lead tire weight. All essential to my success in life at the time.

On the day I was to report to my first day of real "work" I eagerly anticipated the adventure and I glanced at my scratched and scuffed-up Timex watch 1,000 times waiting for the moment when I could "leave for work." I told everyone in my class that I had a job. Some were impressed and some were not. Finally, the time arrived. When the big hand hit the 12 and the little hand was on the 3, I grabbed my "briefcase" and headed towards the big wooden door leading from the classroom and into the cavernous hallway. The only thing between me and my destiny now was two huge metal doors at the end of the hall - I sprinted down the hall, I hit the panic bars and catapulted through the huge doors and ran as quickly as I could down the big hill the school building was built upon.

At the bottom of "school hill," my new career was waiting for me. I carefully looked right, then left, and then right again. No cars were coming, so I held my head high and crossed the street. Walking up the sidewalk to Mr. Mady's office, I walked into the fancy offices with granite floors gleaming and a heavy scent of lemon oil emanating from all of the woodwork and furniture,

Mr. Mady took me out behind the building and pulled a massive Toro Whirlwind lawn mower with a huge engine out of the storage area in the basement. We took it out to the parking lot and loudly and angrily it belched to life after he showed me how to attach the spark plug, prime the engine, and open the choke.

Mr. Mady handed me the controls and showed me how to increase the speed of the engine by pushing the throttle forward. It was a newfangled "self-propelled" model and when you released the handle the mower would leap forward like a wild stallion. At the age of seven with my tiny body and still developing muscles it was all I could do to keep the steed on track.

A week later I came by the office and picked up my very first adult paycheck. I held the big green check in my hand, took it home and showed it proudly to my mother. She took me to the Bank of Virginia. Mom drove me there in our big battleship blue Galaxy 500. We walked into the bank and Mrs. Jones, the bank president, welcomed me into her big office. She gave me some forms and I opened a statement checking account with my first check. She showed me how to write my name on the back of the check and walked me to the front counter of the bank and Miss Sayers took my check and my booklet, wrote something on the statement book and handed it back to me saying "this is the balance in your new checking account." I pocketed the key to my newfound wealth proudly.

However, tragedy struck hard in my young life and career a mere 2 weeks later. After successfully launching my career and earning my second check, Mr. Mady called me into his office. He said solemnly, "Barry, I am sorry son, but we are not going to be allowed to let you mow the grass anymore." I questioned innocently and fearfully, "Did I do something wrong, Mr. Mady...did I do a bad job sir?" Mr. Mady replied, "No son, you did an excellent job, but the government has made a new law and from now on nobody under 18 is allowed to use power tools, so we have to let you go..."

The silence in the room was deafening, and the injustice in my head was maddening...how could it be? (An experience, I would relive many times on my path through life).

126

The words rang in my young head, and I still feel the pain of those six devastating words to this day "we have to let you go…" - but it made no sense whatsoever.

The experience, though tragic to my young heart and mind, I later realized that my father had, through this simple process laid a foundation built on solid bedrock that would serve me for the rest of my life.

Quite simply, without explaining it to me through the introduction to Mr. Mady, I had been given the key that would open many doors for me over the next 50 plus years. The process or formula I now refer to as "Permission, Access, and Profit" has been applied hundreds of times in my life to this date.

Permission refers to the fact that before you can have a conversation with a person and before you can connect with a person, you must have or create permission.

Permission can quickly be gained in any of the following 7 ways:

1) Someone can introduce you to a person and edify or endorse you in the Process.

2) You may explicitly ask permission to contact someone (by asking for their email address, a phone number, or a social media profile URL).

3) You may offer to do them a favor or help with a special project.

4) You could purchase a product or service that allows you to meet the creator.

5) You can just pay directly for the access by booking a consultation (or attend an event where you know the person will be present as a speaker or guest).

6) You can join a mentorship or coaching program where that person is either the mentor or a member of the program.

7) You can just walk up, shake hands with the person, introduce yourself to the person, and casually say "I'd really like to talk with you sometime when you have a few minutes, would that be possible?"

Once you have permission from the person, now you have that all important access.

It's important to realize how valuable access is and to respect the person, and the time of the person who you wish to do business with or interact with.

I made a habit at a very young age of following a simple process to gain the trust, respect, and interest of leaders with whom I wanted to be associated. I call it the 7-minute phone conversation process...

1) I would always start the conversation with a humble, sincere, and heartfelt expression of my gratitude for the few minutes of time that I was granted.

2) I would promise not to take more than 7 minutes of their time.

3) I would keep that promise and that would build trust, so that the next time I reached out to them and asked for 7 minutes of time, then they would trust me and know that I would not waste their time endlessly. Often, I would literally set an egg timer for 5 minutes and do my best to confine that call to 5 minutes instead of seven. When the timer went off, I would say I promised to take no more than 5 minutes of your, time and I have the answers I required, and that bell tells me we have time left over, is there anything else I should know or that you want to share before I hang up...then I'd say thanks again, I really appreciate the time and value that you have shared with me today.

The last step in the process is determining what the next step is that would lead to mutual profit and benefit. To this end, I would always seek to add value to their businesses and their lives by continuously keeping their needs and their business in mind when talking with other people so that I could add extraordinary value with every new conversation.

Years later while working as a newly licensed property and casualty insurance agent for GEICO in their headquarters, I heard the same words again... "we have to let you go..." The words stung just as much then, but this time they only filled me with the resolve to never ever hear those cruel words again.

I set about that day to control my destiny fully, and to never be in a position where another person could ever tell me "We have to let you go."

That set me on a back on my continuing path of self-discovery and adventure and reconnected me with the principles and values that my "Grandaddy" Sterling Johnson and my father Clifton McLawhorn had set me upon many years ago as they instilled their values in me as they groomed me for manhood.

At the age of about 3 or 4 years old my Grandaddy Sterling Johnson took me on his knee and asked me "What you have learned today, Barry?" When I said I don't know Grandaddy, I've just been playing. He said, go get the encyclopedia, learn something, and then come back and tell me what you learned.

I grabbed the World Book Encyclopedia (because we were too poor to afford the Encyclopedia Britannica) and carefully studied something of interest, came back and shared it with my grandfather with bright eyes...

My Grandfather said, "Very good - now, Barry, I want you to remember this - 'A Day on Earth when you have not learned something new is a day of your life wasted,' do you understand me?"

I replied "yes Grandaddy."

To this day at age 61, when I learn something new, especially something unexpected and exciting, I will exclaim - "I've learned something new today, now I can go to bed."

Meet The Author:

Barry C. McLawhorn was "reared" in the heart of the Appalachian Mountains, in the backwoods of Southwest Virginia. He was lovingly mentored, and groomed as a young man, by two towering influences and mentors. The first was his Grandaddy, Sterling Johnson, a C&O Railroad blacksmith and the wisest man to instill lifelong values in his mind and soul when he was still an adventurous and mischievous awe-filled child. The second was his father, Clifton McLawhorn, whom

he says with a gleam in his eye spanked me about three times a day (and, so Barry says, he deserved at least two of those a day - because he was the epitome of the "strong-willed child." Today, at least for the moment, Barry makes his home in the North Georgia mountains and seeks to add extraordinary value to all whose path he crosses.

130

Why I'm Glad I Went Broke

by Mike Molloy

The biggest disaster in my life. And I'm glad it happened. I went broke in 2010 and it was the most embarrassing moment in my life. I never thought I would go broke and just wanted to hide.

I'm getting ahead of myself. Let's go back and see what led to this 'disaster.' Then I'll explain why it was one of the best things that could've happened to me. And how my 'horrible' experience can make you stronger and help you enjoy your life in a way that few people do.

As a kid, I was told to get good grades, go to college, get a good job, get married, and have a family. That was the path to a happy life.

I stayed on that path until 5 weeks into my 2nd year of college. I dropped out. Not because I had bad grades. I didn't feel college was going to take me where I wanted to go. Most people thought I was nuts.

Now I was choosing my own path.

One slight problem …

At 19, I had no clue how to be successful. I had never made more than $10/hr. The first step was to get a job.

My first full-time job, ironically, was in IT for a college. Yes, I dropped out of college and ended up working for a college. This job was fun in the beginning, but I was bored after 3 years. Great lesson as I was considering getting an IT degree.

Then I started a landscaping company. The first year was very messy but I learned a lot. Late in the 4th year of the business, I had to decide whether to scale the small company I had or do something else. I decided to go back to college for mechanical engineering.

I graduated with my bachelor's in mechanical engineering in May 2007 and moved to Missouri for a job as a production supervisor in a cheese manufacturing plant. What a mistake! I lasted 4 months in that job. I chose to resign after a horrible performance review because I already knew at that point it was not the right fit.

I felt like a total failure. What was I going to do now?

It's now October 2007, I'm in a town where I don't know many people and I can't find any entry-level engineering jobs. I decided to continue with the MBA program I started a few months earlier and get a job quickly to cover living expenses. This decision turned out to be a major mistake.

I quickly found a manual labor job, so I didn't put serious effort into finding another full-time permanent job that would use my expertise and skills. I struggled to get by until the end of 2009 when I completed my MBA. Even with the MBA, I only got one job interview and that was arranged by a fellow classmate.

For the next two years, I worked several manual labor jobs including one as a night janitor.

Two college degrees, over $150k in debt,

and I'm working as a janitor for $8/hr. How did I end up here?

In late 2010 my debt load and low income finally crushed me. I defaulted on many debts. I was so scared of all the negative consequences of default. My credit was going to be ruined. I was going to be called by debt collectors. I might be sued by multiple companies. And what will people who know me think of me now that I'm broke?

It wasn't as bad as I feared. I did eventually start receiving a continuous stream of collection phone calls at about 40 per day. My credit was ruined. I continued to work as a night janitor until I got laid off. A week or two later I got sued for the first time in my life by one of my creditors.

It's July 2011 and I'm unemployed and receiving $110 a week for only 16 weeks. I must respond to a lawsuit and can't afford a lawyer. What now? Should I file for bankruptcy? I decided against bankruptcy for the moment unless the situation got to the point where there were no other options.

At this point, the economy was improving, and I was applying for jobs related to my college degrees, but I wasn't getting any interviews.

I was considering moving to Florida to live with my mother. I really didn't want to do this, as it felt like a major step backward. But there is no room for foolish pride when you're broke AND unemployed. Things seemed pretty grim, but I knew they would get better even though I had no clue how that was going to happen.

Signs that it would get better started showing up.

A close friend decided to start a food truck business where he was living in eastern Missouri. He was going to start it in early 2012 and spend the rest of

132

2011 getting everything ready. He invited me to come work for him. I decided to move there at the end of October if I didn't have a job offer.

I did manage to get some interviews in September in Oklahoma, but they didn't lead to offers. I moved in with my friend and left most of my belongings in storage in western Missouri.

Over the next few weeks, I helped my friend build a financial plan for his business and had several more job interviews. A phone interview with a company in Texas went well in early November, and they invited me to fly down for an in-person interview.

I was very excited as this could be my big break!

The interview went very well, and they made an offer the Tuesday after Thanksgiving. I accepted the next day and moved to Houston, Texas a few weeks later.

My early months at this new job as a mechanical design engineer were very difficult. There was a nasty learning curve, and I was working a lot of hours since I knew I needed to get good quickly to deal with my financial mess.

My hard work and focus paid off as I got promoted 18 months later. Only 5 months later I was surprised by an offer to be promoted up 2 more levels to engineering project manager and a salary of just over $100,000. I went from working as an $8/hour night janitor to a six-figure income in just over 2.5 years. This quick ascent at my job did bring new challenges and new gifts, but that is a story for another time.

Going broke was one of the toughest experiences of my life and one of the most valuable ones. I learned a lot and grew much stronger than I was before I went broke. Am I proud of going broke? Absolutely not! I always intended to pay all my debts. It took the experience of making many mistakes and going broke to teach me the following lessons that I'm extremely grateful for.

LESSON 1: Don't focus on making money.

Instead, focus on creating value for others. The making money part becomes fairly easy after this. At my job as an engineer, I was focused on delivering the most reliable tools I could design as fast as I could design them. This required me to develop new skills and strengthen some existing skills. I often asked my boss what he had going on and offered to take on some of his tasks even if I didn't know exactly how to do them. This type of initiative was recognized, and I believe it to be one of the reasons for my quick rise with the company in position and income.

ACTION TO TAKE NOW:

Ask yourself what you are excellent at and how you can use that to create value for others. This will reveal opportunities that make it easy to make money.

LESSON 2: Relationships make almost everything easier.

If I had been better at maintaining relationships, asking for recommendation letters, and connecting with new people when I didn't need a job, it would have been much easier to quickly find a good-paying job. The job I did end up getting as an engineer was through a relative who got my resume to the right people.

ACTION TO TAKE NOW:

Decide on your big goals for the next 5-10 years. Identify people who could help you reach these goals. Start connecting with these people on social media. Build relationships now and figure out how you can help them first. People want to help other people, but they are much more likely to go out of their way to help their friends and family.

This is especially useful for high school and college students. Adults love to help kids.

LESSON 3: All decisions are EMOTIONAL.

We like to think we make rational decisions. That's not how we work. We have a capacity for rational thought that can influence decisions; however, all decisions are rooted in emotion. This explains why we can make choices that seem so illogical. I know from many personal experiences that I made many bad decisions out of fear or anger.

ACTION TO TAKE NOW:

When making decisions, be aware of what you're feeling. It may be useful to consider the decision from a perspective where the emotions are not as strong. The remaining lessons will help you with this.

LESSON 4: All events have value. Even ones we label as negative.

I didn't learn this lesson until sometime after I went broke. Upon reflecting on various events that I had labeled as negative in my life; I realized that each one had given me some kind of gift.

ACTION TO TAKE NOW:

Take any event in your life that you still have very strong 'negative' feelings about. Ask yourself: What did you learn? How am I grateful for this event? This works even better if done in writing by hand. This lesson is one of the most difficult to accept and has been one of the most powerful ones for me.

LESSON 5: We have knowledge, skills, and experience that are very valuable.

Almost everyone undervalues the gifts they have to give. We assume that because something we do is routine or easy for us that it must not be worth much. That is often not true. It is simple to develop valuable skills, and it begins with a mindset of serving (delivering value to others).

ACTION TO TAKE NOW:

What are you excellent at? How does it provide value to others and what can you do to increase this value? Who does it offer the most value to? This will help you identify what to focus on and who can most benefit from the unique value you have to offer.

Read my bio on how to get access to the 2 missing lessons I learned and how they can help you.

Meet The Author:

Mike Molloy has lived in the Houston, Texas area since 2011. He previously lived in Missouri and grew up in Long Island, New York. He has degrees in mechanical engineering and business.

Following a successful 10-year career as a mechanical engineer, he moved full-time into work as Chief Profit Systems Engineer at Evergreen Marketing LLC, a company he founded. Mike focuses on designing and implementing profit systems that bring clients more sales and profits for many years while minimizing risk, cost, stress, and client effort.

He also works part-time as an Elite Mentorship Trainer in facilitating the journey of others through a transformational program/experience he used, and continues to use, to overcome limiting beliefs that were holding him back from living the life he desired.

Mike's business philosophy is that the purpose of business is to improve the lives of people. A big focus of his work with clients is to reduce risk and stress so clients can more fully enjoy growing their businesses.

His primary focus with new clients is to create and install the first profit system for a client and make it profitable for the client in 90 days or less.

If you'd like to see what opportunities for growth are hidden in your business and how to create an infinite marketing budget for your company, then contact Mike at:

https://ProfitSystemsEngineer.com/eh3book

I'll also reveal the 2 missing lessons I learned from going broke.

The 2035 All-Electric Vehicle Illusion

by Anthony Thomas Parker

Are we in the USA positioned to achieve the goal to switch to all-electric vehicles by 2035? I will give you the answer in its simplest form... NO. This goal is the first step in a much broader objective, which is the mandated transformation of our economy to end fossil fuel use, completely eliminate carbon emissions, and establish renewable energy for all economic activity... This is an utter impossibility.

Let's start at the beginning. We must first look at the availability of electricity. All-electric vehicles require substantial charging current (electricity). This electricity must be generated and carried to charging stations as numerous as today's gas stations. This electricity is generated by electrical power plants. New power plants burning coal require about 4-6 years to build. Nuclear plants can take about 7-10 years to complete depending on the location. The US Energy Information Agency (EIA) tells us that wind and solar combined make up 12% of the electricity in the nation's power grid and coal contributes another 22%. The EIA also says that in a few decades, renewables will make up only 38% of the US grid's electricity. Currently, there are no new nuclear power plants likely to be built. And we're shutting down oil and natural gas production across the nation.

So, where will the electrical generation sources come from for the nation? When you buy that electrical vehicle, where will the electricity come from to power it? You must plug your electrical vehicle into something overnight to charge it, or you can't use it the next morning.

The above is the first bare fact that no one wants to talk about. However, without solving this conundrum now, the 2035 goal is only an unsubstantiated dream. Unless we begin a full-scale emergency project to build new power plants, the electrical demand will collapse the power grid. Then, there will be blackouts along with all the other disasters that the collapse will cause. Electricity powers refineries, and refineries make fossil fuel products. Refineries make gasoline for vehicles but also diesel fuel. Diesel fuel is part of the zero CO_2 emission mandate and goal for 2035.

Please think about this for a few moments.

What if there were no tractors to work the crop fields or no farm equipment to grow and harvest our crops? What if there were no ships to move our crops to those countries that we currently trade with?

137

At the moment, about 90,000 ships are sailing the seas. What if there were no eighteen-wheelers to move our food around to the states, cities, towns, and your grocery store? How would you get food to eat?

No diesel fuel means none of these vehicles could operate. It would be impractical to convert tractors, ships, and airplanes to renewable fuels. I remain hopeful that someday these vehicles can be converted to zero-emission fuels, such as hydrogen gas. But not by 2035, as the technology is only in its infancy. Sweden is converting rapidly to hydrogen gas generated from its hydropower plants. But the US would have to build nuclear plants to generate all the needed hydrogen.

Could you envision army tanks and jeeps using batteries? I don't think so. Internal combustion engines using diesel fuel would most likely be required. All those vehicles and vessels use diesel fuel or fossil refinery-based fuels. Today in America's northeast region, there are just seven refineries that produce diesel fuel. There used to be 27. The CEO of Chevron states that there may never be another oil refinery built in the US (Bill Bonner, Founder Agora, Inc). In addition, they're shutting down oil and natural gas production. The government discourages producers of "old energy" while rewarding and subsiding Wall Street and "renewable" sources. Banks will no longer lend to oil and gas companies because it gives them a bad image. So, I ask again, where will the electricity come from for all those electric vehicles needed to replace the current vehicles in the states of California and New York? And what will happen if this dream spreads to all the states in the US? The US will simply not have sufficient electricity generation capabilities and the grid will crash, leaving the country in the dark where crime will abound, and people will fight for food.

Conflicting sources are pushing the global community into a panic mode. Some media authorities predict that "before this cycle is over, gas will hit $50 per gallon, and oil will hit $500 per barrel" (Bonner). It's beneficial to look back at history, as we have previously seen predictions underpinned by threats of doomsday. Have you ever seen the reports and analyses done by Bjorn Lomborg? He is an environmentalist and visiting fellow at Stanford. Time Magazine calls him one of the world's 100 most influential people. And he's repeatedly named one of Foreign Policy's Top Global Thinkers. Lomborg says that New Zealand was the first country to promise a carbon-neutral economy. Their Prime Minister promised a carbon-neutral economy by 2020, which New Zealand failed to achieve with a population about the size of South Carolina. So, they doubled down and reset the goal to 2050 at the cost of $19 billion annually.

But then the cost was reevaluated to $61 billion, which is more than New Zealand spends on social security, welfare, health education, police, courts, defense, environment, and every other part of the government, combined.

Lomborg declares the gas TAXES would need to hit $8.33 per gallon every year for the next 30 years. That is taxes, not including the fuel costs. Lomborg also states that if New Zealand sticks to its plan for the rest of the century, the total amount of greenhouse reduction will deliver a temperature reduction of 0.004 F in the year 2100.

In other words, New Zealand will go bankrupt...and it won't make a dent in the total global greenhouse gas emissions. If we use New Zealand's cost model and apply it to the US, Lomborg says it implies a cost of at least $5 trillion for America in today's money, every single year. Today, the Elite Caste tells us we must make the shift to green energy immediately. It's an emergency, they claim, and U.S. states like California and New York set underthought goals, like no combustion engine vehicles after 2035. Personally, I would bet all I own that this will not happen. Unfortunately, at my age, I wouldn't be around to collect on that bet.

But the Elite Caste has been trying to scare us for decades:

• 1970 – Paul Ehrlich predicted overpopulation would destroy the world.

• 1980 – The UN predicted planetary destruction by the year 2000 due to climate change.

• 2006 – Al Gore predicted world devastation, point-of-no-return in 10 years due to greenhouse gases while he gained about $200 million in net worth.

The biggest CO_2 polluters in the world are China and India. China has no intention to convert to electric vehicles, except to sell them to the US and Europe. I built four coal fired power plants in China and worked there for about four years. I can say they care very little about CO_2 emissions, except when it makes them money. China will supply most of the vehicle batteries to the US. China controls about 80% of

the world's known deposits of lithium and about 60% of the cobalt. These are two mandatory minerals used to make vehicle batteries. Thus, the question is, how do we get China and India to follow the 2035 goal, or for that matter, any CO_2 emission reduction goal? The unfortunate answer is we don't.

Because of the difficulty and cost of obtaining fossil fuels (oil & gas), developing nations are resorting back to burning coal and wood. Coal is readily available in many parts of the world. It has been a struggle to convince those nations to use cleaner fuels. Now, those nations are reverting to what worked many years ago to heat their homes and power their industries: coal and wood. The U.S. is courting Venezuela to supply oil, which is known to be higher polluting. Villages in Germany have timbered some of their local forests to make wood chips to heat their homes, as natural gas is no longer available, and the development of renewable energy sources have been inadequate. Electricity costs are up 87% in Germany compared to a year ago, and natural gas prices are 154% (Bonner). The media makes the argument that electric vehicles are too expensive for the average American. If one leans toward high-end vehicles, this is true. The local Ford dealer is offering the F-150 Lightning truck for about $91,000. But they also have a basic Ford F-150 Lightning electric pickup for $40,000 with an EPA range of 230 miles and 68 MPGe. Compare that to a gas-powered F-150 with a price tag of around $46,000 that gets 15 mpg. It is apparent that the cost of electric cars will not be the insurmountable obstacle to prevent the 2035 goal from being accomplished. Have you ever seen pictures of those old, restored cars in Cuba? Some are real beauties, and they are driven all around the island today. Most of these autos are from 1959, but their owners found some way or another to keep them running well. What do you think the California owners of 17,766,625 autos and the New York owners of 7,870,375 autos will do with the cars they own when the year 2035 comes around?

Will governments condemn these autos, pay to have them "turned in," or will owners continue to repair them as was done in Cuba? Whatever happens, it seems impossible that all these cars will simply disappear. They have value, and there will be a market for them. Most will continue to operate and burn gasoline. There are 129,433,852 cars registered currently in the US according to the US Policy and Government Affairs, Office of Highway Policy Information. Can you see the conundrum here to totally eliminate carbon emissions? The main insurmountable obstacles to achieving the 2035 goal are the lack of basic electrical power generation planned or under construction, an inadequate power grid, and the limitation of US-controlled lithium and cobalt. Unfortunately, politics will have a key bearing on the outcome of the 2035 goal. Gas and diesel-powered vehicles will remain well after the California and New York zero carbon emission goals of 2035.

Renewable energy replacements like solar and wind power will not sustain the power needs of the US, and oil will remain an indispensable need far into the future of the country.

Meet The Author:

Anthony Thomas Parker is a retired engineer who traveled the world and now shares his life experiences through writing all types of content. Mr. Parker holds a master's degree in engineering from Pennsylvania State University and a bachelor's degree in mechanical engineering from the University of Dayton. As a writer, teacher, entrepreneur, engineer, scientist, and executive, Mr. Parker has written all forms of business content. His recent book of poetry, "Life's Poems and their Genesis Stories," is his first personal publication in creative writing. A large portion of Mr. Parker's professional experience was in technical and construction project management of nuclear and fossil power plants, various rocket propulsion systems, petroleum research, marketing, and sales. These projects were located all over the USA, in many foreign countries where Mr. Parker lived and worked from 3–5-year intervals. Thus, he was exposed to business practices, culture, and communication practices in countries such as China, Brazil, Germany, Sweden, The UK, Belgium, Canada, and Thailand. He had to learn to interact and communicate with stakeholders, employees and citizens in each of those countries.

After reinventing himself, now his main focus is writing. His current book, Life's Poems and their Genesis Stories," is currently available on Amazon and Kindle in both eBook and paperback formats. He describes his experiences in love and life with these brilliantly written poems along with inspiring stories behind each writing.

You will laugh, you will ponder, you will cry, you will wonder but most of all, you will be enlightened and entertained in the process. Check out his website at EpicCopyWriter.com. Mr. Parker currently resides in the mountains of Deep Creek, Maryland, which he shares with his son, many deer, mama bears and baby bears, and all the other forest critters! He continues to live life to the fullest and is grateful for each new day!

141

Dare To Grow Rich!

By Michael Penland

I believe in you! I have more faith and confidence in people than they have in themselves. I believe in you because you were born to become an everyday hero. An everyday hero to me is a man or woman placed in an unbelievable situation who takes decisive action to change that situation.

Rather than talk about systems I've created, which have generated over fifty million dollars in revenue, or the wealthy and well-known marketers for whom I worked as a mentor, trainer, or consultant, let me begin by telling you a story from my childhood.

As a small child, I would visit my grandfather on his farm. I enjoyed the visits because my cousins lived on the farm also. During one such visit, one of my cousins told me a story. The story went something like this.

One day as my cousin walked home from school down a dusty old country road, he saw a horse on the side of the road. As would be true for many a young boy, he wanted to take a ride on the horse. Once he was on the back of the horse he said, "Giddy up!"

The horse began walking down that dusty old country road until he came to a big oak tree that had fallen across the road. Because of the obstacle in his path, the horse stopped and just stood there. My cousin gave the horse a gentle kick in the sides and said, "Giddy up!"

The horse went around the obstacle and continued down the path on which he was previously traveling. My cousin told me the ride was a lot of fun until he and the horse came to a crossroads. When this happened, the horse once again stopped dead in his tracks and just stood there. You know what happened next, right? My cousin gave the horse a gentle kick in the sides and said, "Giddy up!"

The horse turned to the right and began walking slowly down the road. As the path began to narrow, the horse started walking faster and faster until he was galloping down the path with my cousin holding on for his life. Then suddenly, the horse swerves off the road to the right and down a driveway past an old farmhouse headed for the barn.

An old farmer came out of the barn and asked my cousin, "How did you know how to get here with my horse?" My cousin answered, "I didn't know, but the horse knew." Today, you may not know the exact path to take to get where you need or want to be. There may be obstacles in the path, and you may find yourself in a situation where you simply don't know which way to turn.

That's OK because this old horse – Michael Penland – knows how to help you get to where you want or need to go. Just hold on real tight for the next few minutes as you continue reading because you're in for the ride of your life. It's time to "Giddy up!"

Listen closely: I wonder if you can imagine what would happen if you were given the power to use every part of your mind for more happiness, more success, and more freedom. How would you feel? What would you see and hear?

If you could have anything in your life bigger, better, or greater, what would it be? Imagine living a life of happiness … success… and freedom! Imagine living the life you want and not the one you've been given.

How To Become Intelligently Ignorant

When I was 17 years old, the son of a tobacco sharecropper from South Carolina with an eighth-grade education taught me how to become intelligently ignorant. Why did I listen to him? I listened to him because he had borrowed $5,000 and turned it into $300 Million in just three years.

Being intelligently ignorant means you're smart enough to become ignorant enough so you don't sit around and try to figure out why something won't work. The only reason one person is making it work and you are not, is that he knows something you don't know, and he takes action.

As a child, I grew up on the wrong side of town… on the wrong side of the railroad tracks. Kids made fun of the clothes I wore and the house in which I lived. Later in life, friends and family made fun of my dream to become a millionaire. They all said, "It won't work." Later they said to me, "It won't last." Now, they ask: "Can you show me how to make the kind of money you've earned?"

If a Miracle Happened in Your Life, How Would You Recognize It?

The American singer-songwriter and philanthropist Bon Jovi said: "Miracles happen every day. Change your perception of what a miracle is, and you'll see them all around you." If a miracle happened in your life, how would you recognize it?

Let me tell you about an everyday hero and a miracle in his life…

A young boy named Tom was born without half of his right foot and only a stub of a right arm. He watched the other children playing sports and wanted so badly to be able to play. Tom especially wanted to play the game of football

144

Young Tom's parents had an artificial foot made for him out of wood and had it encased in a special football shoe. Hour after hour, day after day, little Tom would practice kicking a football with his wooden foot. In his mind, he would try to make field goals. Each time he would attempt to make a field goal at a greater distance. The years passed by, and that little boy named Tom became a young man.

Let your mind travel back in time with me to Sunday, November 8, 1970. You're in the football stadium with 66,910 fans all screaming as the New Orleans Saints battle the Detroit Lions. The score is Detroit 17 and New Orleans 16.

There are only two seconds left in the game and Tom Dempsey with his crippled leg comes onto the field to attempt the longest field goal in football history… a 63-yard field goal. The ball is snapped … placed … and Tom Dempsey kicks and makes a 63-yard field goal. New Orleans upsets and beats Detroit 19 to 17. The six words of losing Detroit coach Joseph Schmidt, when asked about the loss, said it best. He said, "We were beaten by a miracle."

What can we learn from the story of a little boy without half a right foot who would later create a miracle in his life and the life of other people? One lesson is obvious. Spaced repetition of that which he desired resulted in the outcome he achieved. Practice, practice, practice all the processes and action steps I am teaching you right now using spaced repetition. What would happen if every day of every week of every month for the next 12 months you actually did expect a miracle in your life? Would you like to learn how to use your own brain to create a miracle in your life?

21-Day Happiness, Success, and Freedom Secret

When you're dealing with yourself or other people, you do well to ask yourself, "Who do I need to become to get the outcomes I desire?" Think seriously and deeply about this question. Write down, in positively stated details, the answer to that soul-searching question.

Happiness, success, and freedom are all about how you learn to control yourself and you're thinking. It is not about you trying to control other people. Change yourself and others around you will change automatically…or they will leave. Either way, problem solved. Learning to control yourself and your thinking must become a habit. Successful and happy people are simply those who have a life of successful and happy habits.

Your happiness depends upon the habit of mind you cultivate. The Greek philosopher Aristotle said, "We are what we repeatedly do. Success is not an action but a habit." Yes, we first make our habits, and then our habits make us. People don't really decide what their future will be. People only decide what their habits will be, and those habits decide their future.

There are good habits and there are bad habits. A bad habit is like a comfortable bed. It's so easy to get into and so very difficult to get out of. Habits, good or bad, are a product of our own individual choice. Good habits are just as addictive as bad habits, but the outcome is a lot more rewarding.

For most people, it takes 21 days to form a habit. For the next 21 days, I encourage you to do the following three steps to create a miracle in your life and become an everyday hero. This is how habits are formed.

Step #1: Each morning look in the mirror and tell yourself, "I am becoming the person I need to become to get more happiness... more success... and more freedom. Repeat this seven times each morning.

Step #2: Make a list of things for which you are thankful. On day one list seven things for which you are thankful. Add seven additional things each day for 21 days.

Step #3: Help at least one person a day for 21 days enjoy more happiness, success, or freedom. Do this with the words you speak and the actions you take. Remember that there is more happiness in giving than in receiving.

Do these three steps consistently for 21 days and your life will change forever. Also remember this: "Successful people are willing to do for a short period of time what most people are not, so they can do for the rest of their life what most people can't do."

Most Important Question to Ask

Learning how to change your thinking and how you feel about a situation is the secret to more happiness... more success... more freedom. Keep asking yourself: "Who do I need to become in order to get the results and the life I want for myself and my family?" Your answer to this question can be life changing. Don't wish for a miracle in your life; make the miracle happen. To change your life, change the way you're thinking. Don't wish for a better future; change your thinking and create a better future. Learn how to become intelligently ignorant and "Dare to Grow Rich!" You can open the door to more happiness... more success... and more freedom. You can do this. I believe in you!

Meet The Author:

Michael Penland is the creator and founder of "Dare to Grow Rich!" which provides personal development training for individuals and corporations. Recognized as a legendary marketer both online and offline, Michael has trained, mentored and been a consultant for top marketers. Michael has over 50 years in-the-trenches experience and success during which he has created systems which have generated over

$50 Million in revenue. Michael has a burning

passion for helping average men and women achieve extraordinary results in both their business and personal life. People pay $5,700 for his 3-day "Dare to Grow Rich!" personal development workshops which come with a 'Double-Your-Money-Back' Guarantee. After helping hundreds and hundreds of attendees, no one has ever asked Michael to honor the guarantee.

Having mastered the skills of copywriting, sales, marketing, and SEO, Michael Penland has discovered how to transfer these skill sets to other people through powerful mindset development training. Michael wants you to have a special gift which reveals secrets responsible for $500,000,000.00 in revenue. It's available FREE at https://www.daretogrowrich.com/500-million

The Key to Success!

By Michael Powell

Hello, how many of you have a dream that you want to accomplish? Let me tell you something. One of the things I want you to consider right now is your dream. Because I want to show you how to start seeing the world on your terms, from a point of view that will enrich your life. This is the story of Willie Author Powell, who was born in a house in the backwoods of Rochelle, Georgia. On December 2, 1938, from Eugene Powell and Lulma May Powell. Could you picture what would be going through your mind right now if you were a father and your child was born at home by a midwife rather than in a hospital with a doctor? And, if you're a mother, what will be going through your mind as you give birth to your child in a house?

Willie is the second oldest of ten children. Yes, I did say ten children, five boys: Fayette, Willie, Edward, Jerome, and Clinton and five girls: Lula, Dorothy, Pauline, Susan, and Shirley. Willie began working in the cotton fields of Georgia with his father and some of his siblings at the age of 13. They would travel back and forth between Georgia and Florida, picking cotton in Georgia and beans in Florida. Where the sun shines brighter than a thousand rays bursting through the clouds, it must be the sun's way of dancing alone. Willie would wrap a sack around his shoulders, much like a satchel, and then begin working on a row, separating the stem from the cotton or bean to fill the sacks.

The process doesn't end with one sack; he must keep filling them up until his father says they are entirely filled. How long do you think it would take to get enough cotton or beans to feed your family if you started at 3 a.m. and finished at 5 p.m.? I can see why my father always said that we don't understand what hard work is. But the irony is that I believe I am the hardest-working man on the planet. Eugene Powell eventually left Georgia and moved his family to Florida. Eugene paid for a three-bedroom house with one bathroom so that his family could have a place to live. Willie would graduate from Roosevelt High School in 1957.

Willie started working for the town of Palm Beach County in 1960, when he was 22 years old, doing lawn work. The days were hot and humid. As the workers work, steam can be seen coming off their heads. You swear the devil was standing right next to you.

Willie continued to work with the town of Palm Beach as the days passed. But on this particular day, Willie was summoned to clear the palm tree limbs from the ground beneath the palm tree his uncle was cutting. Don't blink or bat an

149

eye because you're about to lose your apple pie. The hatchet slips from his uncle's grasp and slow motion begins to set in as the hatchet falls. Whoosh, whoosh, whoosh.

Willie is struck in the head with the hatchet, and blood begins to flow everywhere. They wrap his head, but the blood still pours like a river flowing downstream. Willie is rushed to St. Mary's Hospital after 911 is called. Willie survived because God is good; if it had been 2 inches to the left, he would not have survived.

Willie and his older brother Fayette were drafted into the army the following year, on November 20, 1961. And one of his younger brothers, Edward, enlisted at the same time as his older brothers.

Willie learned how to work in avionics while in the army; his job was to repair radios so pilots could communicate with air traffic control. Willie worked his way up the ranks from PFC (Private First Class) to staff sergeant. Willie was overjoyed when his first child, Diep, was born on June 17, 1967, while he was in Vietnam. Diep's mother eventually gave up Diep to the convent (orphanage) because she no longer wanted to care for her.

Willie had made numerous attempts over the years to remove his daughter from the orphanage. But he was at a loss because children born from interracial relationships were not accepted in Vietnam. Willie, on the other hand, went to see her whenever he could.

Willie would fall head over heels in love with his secretary. She was quite a sight. He used to follow her around everywhere, looking for a date. (I can say that my father is persistent.) Nguyet eventually caved and they began dating.

Years passed, and on July 10, 1969, Willie resigned from the army and returned to the United States. Willie quickly returned to Vietnam on a mission to get his daughter out of the orphanage. And to propose to the woman he loved.

Willie asked her to marry him several times, but she always said no. However, on November 3, 1973, at 1:00 p.m. their son, Tony Powell, was born. When Diep saw her baby brother, she called him her "baby."

Willie then decided one day, "This is the last time I'm going to ask this lady to marry me." I told you he's persistent and never gives up. She finally told him that she would marry him and that she was ready.

Because many of the children in the orphanage were the offspring of soldiers who had babies in Vietnam, the non-profit organization All Children arranged to bring them back to the United States.

Willie once heard a small still voice tell him not to put his daughter on that plane. But he was overjoyed to finally be able to bring his daughter home. He never listened to the voice that told him not to put his daughter on that plane. Diep was ready to go, and on April 4, 1975, it was time to bring the children to the United States.

Willie would never see his daughter's face again. The plane crashed in Saigon. On April 16, 1975, Willie and Nguyet married. And left Vietnam on April 23, 1975, to return to the United States. Then, on August 5, 1975, they left the United States for Iran, where they stayed for four years before returning to the United States in 1979. Willie was employed by Augusta company (an Italian helicopter manufacturer) and relocated his family to Saudi Arabia in 1979.

When Nguyet was pregnant, Tony prayed for a baby brother and not a sister, and God heard his prayers because he gave him two brothers, one on February 10, 1980, at 5:00 p.m. when Danny Powell was born. And 9 months later at 5:00 a.m. on January 1, 1981, their baby boy Michael Powell was born.

After living in Saudi Arabia for 8 years on January 7, 1987, Willie brought his family back to the United States. Willie would do everything for his children, including attending baseball and football games. Willie encouraged his children to pursue their dreams. All he asked was that if you want to do something, you do it to the best of your ability.

Willie was a family man who raised his children in a traditional way. And if you're not familiar with the old-school method, let me explain. In one word, whoopins, whoopins, and more whoopins. When Willie was younger, anyone could give him a whoopin. When I say everybody, I mean everyone, like teachers and the entire neighborhood.

Willie would tell his children, "I will whoop you from the youngest to the oldest, from the smallest to the tallest." But if my father was telling this story, he would say he never whooped us. Because, in his mind, his whoopins paled in comparison to the whoopins Eugene Powell gave him and his siblings. If you got bad grades in school, read incorrectly, or talk back...whoopin. You might have gotten a whoopin if you even sneezed wrong.

Willie put the fear of God in his children to the point where their friends did something wrong. Willie's children's spider sense would go off in their heads. If your father finds out, he will kill you, says a small still voice. And these folks kept us out of a lot of whoopins and out of jail.

Nguyet is the common thread that runs through this family. Without her, the kids would have thought their father was going to kill them with all those whoopins.

Nguyet used to stand behind Willie and save the day by explaining the correct spelling to Tony when his father asked him how to spell a word. Nguyet was learning how to spell words at the same time as Tony.

Danny and Michael, on the other hand, were like two peas in a pod; whenever one got a whoopin, the other got a whoopin. When Nguyet began to cry, Willie would stop whooping them. But when the kids got out of hand, she'd tell Willie about it, and Willie would hand out whoopins like they were going out of style.

Nguyet was the type of mother who was willing to ride and die for her children. It made no difference where the kids were in the world; if they were in danger, she would be on the next plane smoking.

Willie would instill in his children the skills and values required for success. Willie often told his children that whatever a man thinks, that is what he will become. He would teach them that their mind is the most powerful thing on the planet and that anything is possible in this world if you put your mind to it. Willie, 83, has dementia and can't remember what happened 5 or 10 minutes after you speak to him. But let me tell you how powerful the mind is. Willie struggled to recall the name of his grandchild's wife. When his grandson Anthony and his wife Natalya visited, he always asked what his wife's name was. When she inquired, he always replied, "Anthony's wife." As a result, my brothers and I, as well as my mother, were constantly reminding him that her name was Natalya. He eventually remembered her and can still recall her name.

I'm sharing this story with you because if my father had not had the fortitude and mental toughness to overcome prejudice, the death of his daughter, and many other challenges in his life, it might not have transpired as it did. I wouldn't be sharing his story either. So, I am leaving you with this. Here is a pro tip from one of my mentors Caleb O'Dowd: The reality is the journey to success is an internal journey. It's you who are doing work on yourself to get the best out of yourself.

Meet The Author:

Michael Powell is the CEO and Founder of Black Lotus Marketing Solutions. What is Black Lotus Marketing Solutions all about? We are a marketing firm that will work for you for free. We identify your problems and we've developed a solution that far outperforms all previous products, courses, and programs you have paid for in the past. But instead of wasting your time and money on tactics that may or may not work for you

We introduce you to some of the top super affiliate marketing programs available today. That has been tried and tested and is supported by actual data. Every day, our goal is to help as many people as we can in going above and beyond what others have done in order to build an unstoppable profitable internet business. So that anyone from 10 to 90 years old can learn how to run their own successful internet business without all the nonsense.

Michael Powell is part of an elite group of entrepreneurs who help people launch and grow their internet dream business so they can achieve what others believe is impossible. However, the past year and a half Michael Powell has been experiencing one of the most life-changing experiences he's ever had. Michael Powell has been putting in the time and money to find just the right approach to help people develop and grow their business.

Working with some of the industry's top super marketers like:

Anthony Morrison / Vick Strizheus / Mark Lack / Ryan Levesque / Matt Bacak / Caleb O'Dowd / Grant Cardone

Invested over 50k in his affiliate marketing education.

And made a home on the internet for people to be connected to some of the top super affiliate marketing programs where they can be nurtured, grow, and develop their skills in marketing so they can build their dream business online. But the best part that comes with his business is when he is able to help folks with their problems. He truly realizes the true importance of affiliate marketing and the positive impact it can have on people's lives.

Michael's Free Bonus:

https://blacklotusmarketingsolutions.com/mass-traffic-blueprint-2

Shivaji: The Warrior of Western India

by Ani Railkar

For hundreds of years, the Western Indian state of Maharashtra was tormented by invaders. They would tear down temples, loot and kill innocent people, and rape and kidnap women and girls. The citizens of Maharashtra were tired of this oppression. They prayed to the Goddess Bhavani for help. Their prayers were answered on February 19, 1630, when a son, Shivaji was born to Jijabai and Shahaji Bhonsle. Busy fighting for the Sultan of Bijapur, Shahaji was not there to welcome his son.

Since Shahaji was always away, Shivaji learned how to read, write, use weapons, and ride a horse from his tutor, Dadaji Konddeo. Jijabai told him stories from mythology and history. Early in his life, Shivaji and his followers took an oath to free his people from the oppressive rule of the invaders. As he grew older, he built a small army and started capturing forts belonging to the Sultan. He used guerilla warfare and lightning strikes to catch the enemy by surprise. As punishment, the Sultan ordered one of his generals-Afzal Khan, to capture Shahaji. Afzal Khan marched against Shivaji with a huge force. Shivaji pretended to be scared and asked for a meeting. From his spies, he had learned that Afzal Khan was going to kill him during the meeting. Shivaji was prepared, he turned the tables on Afzal Khan and killed him instead.

He was attacked by Siddhi Johar, another Bijapur general, but Shivaji managed to evade him.

To fund his fight, Shivaji attacked Surat, a lucrative port belonging to the Mughal Emperor Aurangzeb. Aurangzeb sent his uncle Shahista Khan against Shivaji. He came to Pune and stayed at Shivaji's childhood home Lal Mahal. Disguised as a wedding party, Shivaji attacks Shahista Khan, but lets him go with three fingers missing. Enraged, Aurangzeb captured Shivaji under the guise of friendship. But Shivaji managed to escape unharmed. As soon as he reached Pune, he declared himself the King of Independent Maharashtra.

Shivaji was a one-of-a-kind hero. Despite being Hindu, he employed people of all faiths. Whenever he attacked the enemy, he never harmed women and children. Inspired by him, many other states fought against invaders for independence.

Meet The Author:

Ani Railkar is an international award-winning author, coach, mentor and entrepreneur. Dr. Railkar was born and brought up in Mumbai, India. After getting his BSc degree in Chemistry from the University of Bombay, India, he came to the US. He has a MS in Pharmaceutical Sciences from West Virginia University in Morgantown, WV. He has a PhD in Pharmaceutical Sciences from the University of the Sciences in Philadelphia. Dr. Railkar has worked in the pharmaceutical industry for 25 years. He has published six books, written book chapters and has been published in peer reviewed scientific journals. He has written the award-winning book The Great Testosterone Myth: Honest Facts No Hype. If you are a man over 30 and would like to know your testosterone type, take the quiz here: https://quiz.thedrani.com/sf/64e51cc7.

He currently lives in Ambler, PA with his family. Find out more about Dr. Railkar at www.anirailkar.com or email ani@anirailkar.com.

Preston's 7 Master "C" Words to Success

by Preston Rahn

Success is defined as an accomplishment or desired achievement. Over my many years of working with top successful people and helping people become successful with money, relationships, health and generally in their life, I find that success comes down to a few key words. When you focus on the following words you will see more success. If you feel sick, you want to feel better. In work, you want to do a better job. In a relationship, you want to have a better connection or experience more love. And with money, you want to have a better bank account.

We all want to get better and improve our lives. No one says they are doing something to make it worse or to feel worse or to live worse off than they are now. And success is not an end goal or the desired achievement but it's really enjoying the journey on the path we travel. True success is when you can feel satisfied with where things are now, knowing that things could always be better or worse and that tomorrow is another day to enjoy the journey.

On my path, I've come up with a few key "C" words that can help you to focus on improving and getting better in every area of your life. Here they are...

1. Change

In order to get from where you are to where you want to be you must change and change is just a choice to do something differently than you've been doing. The definition of insanity is doing the same thing and expecting a different result. So, to expect a different result you must do what you've been doing differently.

If you aren't feeling satisfied with where you are or not comfortable with the results that you've been experiencing, then you must become aware of how things are. If you don't feel satisfied with how things feel or your perception of how things seem to you now, you can choose to do something differently so you can experience a different result or outcome.

2. Communication

The way you communicate with others will determine how they respond to you. Communication is how you interact with others and how you also communicate with yourself. Communication is not just the words you say but also the way you say them. You can communicate in a conversation, but you can also communicate with your body language and not just with words.

How you feel can also alter the things you say and how you say or communicate them. So, be aware of how you feel when communicating because it can alter the way others, and yourself, interpret what you are trying to convey and cause confusion and contrast or clarity.

3. Clarity/Contrast/Confusion

Being clear with how you communicate is also important because if you aren't clear, then you can confuse the person you are communicating with, and you can also become confused too. When you are not clear with what you are saying or with the message you are conveying, your results can conflict with the way you thought they would turn out. In addition, when you are not clear, you can make less than ideal decisions or fail to decide all together and not know what to do next on your path to success.

Napoleon Hill, in chapter 8, Decision, of his book, Think and Grow Rich, said that after analyzing over 25,000 men and women "that lack of decision was near the head of the list of the thirty major causes of failure." He also said, "People who fail to accumulate money, without exception, have the habit of reaching decisions, if at all, very slowly, and changing these decisions quickly and often." When you are clear, you can make quick decisions and making quick decisions is a big factor in achieving success.

One thing to realize, though, is that if you are not experiencing things going the way that you want them to be going, then making a change is important. One thing I often say when things don't seem to be going well is, "What's the opposite of that?"

Contrast and Confusion are the opposites of clarity and one thing I often say is "Contrast provides clarity." The contrast you experience will provide the clarity needed to see things in a new way, to see what you do want and pave the path for you to experience something different. So, just because something isn't going the way you want it to go or the way you expected it, embrace that confusion and contrast because in seeing what you don't want you can become clear in seeing and experiencing what you do want.

4. Consistency

Being consistent with what you think, say, do and believe can also help you to make quicker and better decisions.

Being consistent can either help you succeed or aid in your failure. If things are getting better for you then being consistent will help you to continue to get better and better results. And, if things aren't going well or not getting better for you then being consistent can hurt or even cripple your decision-making ability and your future success.

5. Commitment

Commitment is your level of dedication to achieving a goal, a cause, an idea, an activity or even your level of dedication to a person. It's your sustained level of effort or persistence. Most people will give up at the first sign of an issue or problem. But those who are 100% committed will continue on despite the contrast that they see.

When we date someone or marry someone, we commit to only being with them. When someone asks us for help, we commit to helping them and being there for them. Commitment is really doing what you say you are going to do, whether to yourself or to another. And it's usually easier to commit to another person rather than making a commitment to ourselves. Just look at a New Year's resolution that you make. How long does that commitment last? Usually, not very long.

If success were easy though, then everyone would be successful. Those that experience success persist through the contrast and that persistence comes down to their level of commitment. Following the previous 4 steps will help you to stay committed and not give up on your goals and dreams.

6. Convictions/Core Beliefs

In the last step, commitment is more of an action that you do, and conviction is defined as a firmly held core belief or the quality of showing that one is firmly convinced of what one believes or says. So, Conviction is what you believe at your core level and your core belief is the key behind true success because you get what you believe. If you believe that it takes hard work to succeed you will most likely experience things being hard. But if you believe that it is easy and things don't have to be hard to succeed, things will most likely come easy for you. Success really can be that simple.

I believe that things always work out for me and that things come easy for me and for the most part, they do. I believe that we create our own reality, that there's no need to worry or doubt and that we can create any life that we want to. I believe in having faith that things work out and not focusing on the contrast. And that leads us to my 7th C word, Create or Creation.

7. Create/Creation

My conviction, or belief is that we all have the ability to consciously and deliberately create our reality because you get what you think about most often and what you believe. You can create the life you want based on your convictions or core beliefs, but chances are that you haven't been communicating out very clearly what you want to experience.

Most people react to what they see and experience, which is usually what they don't want. That focus creates more of what you don't want to experience, and people wonder why what they do want doesn't come. You have to focus on what you do want in order to receive it. Focusing on the contrast creates more contrast. The "language" you communicate out is how you ultimately create your reality. So, try focusing on what you want to create and then expect it to come.

8. Bonus... Coaching/Consulting

It's hard to do it all on your own. When you want to make a change and experience success in your life it's much easier to do it with someone who has been there and done it and who has helped others to do it. This is why hiring a Coach or Consultant to help you improve are my Bonus "C" words for you.

Even the most successful people that I know hire other people to help them succeed in some area of their life. Top Athletes hire people to help them improve and stay at the top of their game. Businesspeople hire financial planners to help them improve their investments and financial life. Other people hire people to help them with their health and weight, relationships, home remodeling, hair, skin, marketing, and even life coaches are hired to give advice, to help improve people's lives and to experience more success in their life. Ultimately, people hire other people to feel better, to feel more satisfied and to experience the feeling of success.

As you can see, these "C" words will help you to stay on track to experience more success in your life. In order to feel better and get better we must move past the resistance. The less resistance and negative things we feel the better we will get and the better we will feel. I know it sounds simple but sometimes people make things more complicated than they need to be. The less resistance you experience and the more you feel better, the better your life will become. Some things are easier than others and some things will take years to overcome but that really comes down to what you believe at your core.

Success is an ongoing process and when you discover what you want, and you believe it is possible you can become successful at anything in your life and live a life that you are satisfied with.

If you want help creating a new reality and experiencing more success in any area of your life then contact me and let's Communicate, have a Conversation and see if there's a fit because I am happy to help you create and experience more success in any area of your life.

Meet The Author:

Preston Rahn is a coach, consultant and #1 bestselling author who helps people experience more success in their life. He primarily helps people experience more sales and money in their business but really all success comes down to focusing more on what you do want, rather than focusing more on what you don't want. His core belief is that everything works out for us, if we believe that, because we get what we believe and focus on. He also believes that we create our own reality and helps people to do just that. If you would like help creating a new reality in your life and experiencing more happiness, joy, love, health, money and overall satisfaction in your life, contact Preston through his social media channels on LinkedIn.com or Facebook.com. Just send him a message and let him know that you found out about him through this book, Everyday Heroes.

How I Sold 70,000+ Products Online Using Free Traffic

By Marlon Sanders

Let's talk about selling products online.

I've sold 70,000+ products online.

Most of those were over $50.00 each.

In the following pages, I hope to shine a light on your path and show you step-by-step how you can also sell products online.

Or, if you're already doing it, how you can sell MORE products online.

Keep in mind that while these are my experiences, they aren't typical nor indicative of average results. You could do better, worse, or nothing at all. That's the life of an entrepreneur.

A Quick Summary of How I Got Here
Starting from Pennies

One time I had to pay for deodorant with only pennies. I had a car that smoked like a bomb. Yet, I scraped together every dime and nickel I had to buy books and courses that would give me the secrets of selling. I was determined yet

disappointed by some of the things I'd tried that were real stinkers.

Like my first info product How to Avoid TV Repair Rip-off. I made the classic mistake of selecting that product that many newbies make. Can you spot why it was a total zero?

Anyway, I kept on and sooner or later, it paid off. And when I say paid off, let me give you really, hard numbers.

Here are the monthly gross sales I had back then, beginning in March of 99.

$23,254.99

$47,093.18

$49,949.95

$42,288.42

$45,161.60

$32,670.86

19,646.07

$23,923.07

$23,373.40

$25,900.62

Not too shabby when most people at the time were still trying to figure out what a domain name was. Or you can go back to 1996. I'm looking at my bank statement with deposits of $18,994.35. Or 12-17-1996 deposits of

$12,866.38. And so forth. Back then, part of my income was also from speaking and writing. But the point is, I've been making real money on the Internet for longer than most.

And I've been doing numbers like those, or better, ever since. For most of those

years, I did it from my home office with only a few virtual staff.

I have a long history of numbers like those or better, year after year, with 19 breakthrough products like these: Gimme My Money Now, How To Create Your Own Products In A Flash, Marketing Dashboard, Design Dashboard, Cash Like Clockwork, Action Grid, Automation Secrets, Website Tricks, Push Button Letters, PR Cash, Web Site Order Taking Machine, Internet Profits Explosion Club, How To Write Killer Copy, How to Go From Broke To Prosperity, Product Dashboard, VBlog Secrets, Marketing Diary, Amazing Formula, Red

Factor, and that's the short list. It doesn't include coaching programs I've done, participation in other people's products, or some of my lesser-selling products.

I've cranked out winner after winner for years. It's one thing to be a Johnny one-hit-wonder. And quite another to do it year after year. Most people would be ecstatic to have just one or two of those products on their resume.

The One Book That Changed My Life

In 1978 I ordered a book from an ad that said, "Ohio Man Discovers 7 Step System to Escape the Rat Race," or something like that.

He filled out forms in the comfort of his RV vehicle. And all this money came flooding in.

I thought that sounded good!

The book introduced me to direct response marketing and also a guy named Gary Halbert who Ben Suarez, the author of the book, had worked with.

I fell in love with a thing called "direct response marketing."

I piddled around and did my best to sell products through little $5 and $10 ads. I ran an ad in TV guide to sell a booklet on how to avoid TV repair rip-off.

Why anyone would be reading a TV guide if their TV was broken is beyond me! Needless to say, I had a LOT to learn.

Fast forward several years and the Internet came along. I began marketing on AOL and CompuServe.

Eventually, I stumbled across a FORMULA for selling eBooks online. I contend I was the first person to sell 100% digitally delivered eBooks online via an affiliate program.

Certainly, I was one of the first.
The formula was simple:

eBooks + 100% digital delivery + 12-step sales page + online order form + affiliate program

When I discovered the formula, money started pouring in $20,000, $30,000,

$40,000 a month.

The money poured in...

My affiliates raked in thousands in commissions.

Getting to the total number of products I've sold isn't easy. You have to add

numbers from multiple accounts.

I'm NOT showing you ANY of this to brag.

There are so many people today claiming to be experts, I just wanted to show you I know a thing or two about selling online.

So, Marlon, How Did You Sell Those Products?
As I said, I had a formula:

eBooks + 100% digital delivery + 12-step sales page + online order form + affiliate program

1. eBooks – When I started, everyone was shipping printed books.

The common thinking at the time was if you sold a digital-only product, your refunds would be through the roof.

I've heard of people selling eBooks back on the bulletin board systems. So, I

can't say I had the first eBooks. But far as I know, no one, or almost no one, was doing it at the time of WWW.

In any event, this formula STILL works, but things have evolved.
I STILL sell eBooks for up to $100.

But what works better is to COMBINE elements.

Combine a PDF with some videos and other doodads.
Maybe you have templates, checklists, or other items.

This makes it impossible to compare your value with all video products sold on Udemy for 10 bucks or Kindle books sold for $2.

I didn't think of this idea. Dan Kennedy originally came up with the idea pre-www. He would ship you this ugly notebook with cassette tapes stuffed in the front, certificates for consultations, and other stuff. It was a monstrosity! But you sure as heck couldn't compare the value to a "book." The enemy of profits is commoditization.

In other words, having your products relegated to the status of a commodity like apples or oranges. Everyone knows how much an apple, or an orange is worth. Not much. This is a HUGE problem with platforms like Udemy and Amazon Kindle. They turn your intellectual property into a commodity. There ARE ways to break out of this trap. And those platforms have their uses. But, in general, today you sell a collection of value, NOT just an eBook. Although you can sell just eBooks. I do it by having extremely strong sales copy with big promises.

2. 100% Digital Delivery
That was element two.

Back then, it was a big deal. Today, it isn't. People today get excited about

selling and shipping ecomm products out of their garages. What a nightmare!

I've been there and done that with CDs and manuals. Hated it.

So, we'll move on.

3. 12-Step Sales Page

This is a critical part of the puzzle. I was a copywriter for Phil Kratzer (a guru of the day) at National Response Corporation in Dallas, TX on Inwood Drive. Gary Halbert used to fly in weekly to meet with Phil.

Remember that I had read about Gary Halbert in the 1978 book. So, when I had a chance to write for a guy who knew Gary Halbert, I jumped at the opportunity!

Phil sold a book on copywriting by a fellow named Bob Serling. Bob had this 16-step (or more) copywriting formula. It was the FIRST time I saw anyone codify a sales letter into a step-by-step formula. This changed my life. I took Bob's lengthy formula, extracted the elements that were most important to me, and created a 12-step formula. Before I developed this formula, the best thing you had was AIDA, which stands for attention, interest, desire, action.

Boiled down, that means you have a headline, then talk about a problem you solve or opportunity you have for the reader, you present the solution and then have a call to action, often with bonuses and a deadline. The problem is, it's hard to conceptualize a whole sales letter that really works based on that

formula. You can do it. But it's not easy. My formula broke things down a lot more.

A lot of people write sales copy based on what other people do. But they don't really understand the PSYCHOLOGY behind it. You can START with understanding that almost all sales offers are simply presenting an idea on how to solve a problem or take advantage of an opportunity. That's all you're doing in sales. You're presenting ideas to people that help them solve a problem or take advantage of an opportunity. People have a lot of misconceptions about sales. You start with this fundamental. You're NOT shoving stuff at people.

You're helping people solve problems or capitalize on opportunities they're

interested in.

4. Online Order Form

I use several systems today to take orders. Thrivecart and Warriorplus.com. Those are the main two. Automateyourwebsite.com is my private label and also has a shopping cart built into it. It's an all-in-one system that has a lot of great features at a very reasonable price. There are a million and one shopping carts. The most popular one works with WordPress and is called Woo commerce. I'm not that big a fan of it, but a lot of people love it.

5. Affiliate Program

You need traffic. That is visitors to your sales page. Eyeballs on your offer. Today, there are MANY options, like YouTube videos, Quora, Facebook organic posts or paid ads, and many more, including an affiliate program. I write a weekly newsletter to help affiliates make sales and money. This is also one way I attract affiliates to promote my offers. The great thing about an affiliate program is that just 1 affiliate who promotes your offer can send you a lot of sales. You don't pay until AFTER the sales.   And it's all AUTOMATED.

Forexample, one time on a Friday night, someone decided to promote an offer of mine. And that weekend something on the order of $90,000 in sales came in. That's quite unusual, of course. But you never know. Here's a big tip: Put your link to your affiliate info page at the bottom of your sales pages where affiliates can see it. You'll have affiliates click that link and sign up if they like your

product. There's a lot more to tell you about how to succeed using this formula. I haven't talked about list building, your email list, target marketing, or other things.

Meet The Author:

Marlon Sanders innovated a number of techniques that are now commonplace online, including the 12-step formula for writing sales letters, 2-page web site model, structure of modern download pages, and the list goes on and on. He was a major contributor to what is just accepted practice in today's Internet marketing.

The seminars he spoke at in Boulder, Colorado with Jonathan Mizel and Declan Dunn hold a special place in Internet marketing lore and were attended by many who went on to become Internet marketing "gurus."

In fact, he has spoken at seminars with Jeff Walker, Yanik Silver, Jeff Paul, Bill Glazer, Andrew Reynolds, Russ Brunson, Armand Morin, Alexandria Brown, David Cavanaugh, Ted Ciuba – and many others.

In addition, he has spoken at over 120 seminars around the world including Australia, Bermuda, Kauai, London and Birmingham in the UK, and all over the U.S. -- including Seattle, San Francisco, Las Angeles, St. Louis, Chicago, Nashville, Philadelphia, San Diego, Houston, Dallas, Sacramento, New York, and Cincinnati.

He has shared the platform with Corey Rudl, Armand Morin, Yanik Silver, E. Joseph Cossman, Dan Poynter, Ted Nicholas, Ted Ciuba, Robert Allen, Jim Edwards, Alli Brown, and dozens of others. His products are used by thousands around the world in 72+ countries.

With the help of Paul Myers and a long list of contributors, he played a crucial role in rallying the troops to speak out to the FTC about proposed legislation concerning the Can Spam law as it influenced affiliate, He was a featured at the Next Internet Millionaire seminar produced by Joel Comm and has had the honor and pleasure of speaking at Big Seminar not once but twice and most recently spoke at Frank Garon's event in London.

Marlon invented several product categories that have become popular such as Push-Button Letter Generators and Dashboards of various types. He's perhaps most known for The Amazing Formula That Sells Products Like Crazy which was one of the first digitally delivered eBooks on Internet marketing to capture the attention of the marketplace.

Marlon's affiliate program for his products has appeared numerous times in the top 10 list at associateprograms.com, and Amazing Formula was in the Mensa online catalog for people with genius IQ's.

Noah And Her Ark

by Koni Scavella

When the phone rang that afternoon, I was tempted not to answer it.

There was no caller ID.

Odd…I thought to myself.

As my thumb moved to tap the red hang-up icon, a small voice inside called out to me.

Wait.

Take this call.

I wasn't expecting a call from a hero that day. But it would be nice.

I live in a small, southern California beach town that, quite frankly, doesn't get much action.

Is it just my hot-blooded Italian-German nature, or are we all slightly intoxicated by the larger-than-life, mythical hero?

When DC Comics ™ and Marvel™ feed us the daring adventures of Captain America, Thor, The Flash, Ironman, and the like, we feel inspired to greatness.

But sometimes the small, frail, silent heroes stir something even deeper in us.

These unsung heroes have spent a lifetime on the battlefield. They carry the wounded on their back. They work into the night without complaint. And they rarely come home to applause or a parade.

When in the presence of one, you may not recognize them at first. They are not the adrenalin-filled conquerors driven to win as much as they are quiet ambassadors drawn by an inner calling to serve.

But who is calling me now?

After I said hello, there was silence.

Hmmm…

Perhaps it's Spiderman. He doesn't speak much.

I repeated myself. A little louder this time.

"Hello?"

The voice was hesitant. Soft. Polite.

169

The caller knew me, but did I know her?

There was an odd familiarity to the gravelly voice. But from where?

My researchers' brain instantly went into my historic archives, searching through trillions of bits of information in search of a match. Nothing.

I pulled the phone from my ear and looked at it as if I could find more clues on the blank screen.

"Who is this?"

"It's Angie," she said as if I may recognize her...but still a bit unsure of herself. Angie... I silently contemplated.

My brain was now on high alert. Like an intern running behind his boss who shoves that much-needed file at her in the last seconds before she enters the boardroom, my hippocampus quickly retrieved a memory of the only Angie I knew and slapped up an image on my mind.

But I rejected it. This is not her.

That Angie was fierce. Her life functioned like a well-oiled machine. She was quick-witted, street-smart, and business savvy. Best of all, she was smooth as silk with clients.

Her given name was not accidental. She was an angel to so many people, and everyone loved being near her.

I affectionately gave her the nickname Noah. It was a biblical reference to the story of Noah and the Ark. You see that Angie had a heart bigger than the earth's circumference.

She would see someone in need and help them out. She had a particularly soft spot for animals and would bring them onto her Ark, two- by-two.

Eventually, her success allowed her to buy a beautiful 5-acre farm in the country for all her strays. Over the years, she fostered 20 kids, adopted 6 special needs kids, and filled the Ark with 4 horses, 2 goats, 16 dogs, 12 cats, one wolf, an African parrot, a bird, 3 ferrets, 50 chickens, and the occasional reptile.

Since she lived in rainy Washington state, the Noah and the Ark reference was even more apropos.

That Angie was the rock of her family. She was loving, and overly generous to family and friends, leaving no one in her presence wanting for anything. While her kids had everything, they were never raised with a sense of entitlement.

She married her high school sweetheart, but they couldn't have children of their own. Angie never complained. She was often plagued with illness, but it didn't stop her.

It was at this point in her life that our business paths crossed.

I owned a very successful mortgage company and real estate investment firm. We were rapidly expanding into 13 states, and I needed an operational genius to handle our processing division.

Angie came without any experience but had everything I was looking for. With the Noah effect in full force, we scaled to a 65% referral business and became the #1 brokerage in a year. I was able to travel extensively, only working on my business 4-6 months per year, thanks to Angie at the helm.

It was a great life for all of us.

I sold the business prior to the mortgage meltdown in 2008. After cashing out, Angie and I went our separate ways. She started her own company, and I eventually went on to writing books, consulting, and speaking.

I confess, I often wished she was with me again at The Iconic Brands. She would have been the perfect fit.

My brief trip down memory lane came to an abrupt halt when the caller spoke again.

"Koni, this is Angie, from the mortgage days."

"This is THAT Angie?" I asked incredulously.

"I couldn't recognize you. You don't sound like you at all. How are you?" I asked as a big smile returned to my face.

It faded just as quickly when she spoke.

"I am not doing well. I need your help. Everything has fallen apart. I lost everything. I haven't even felt like going on. If it weren't for my new son, I don't think I would be here."

I sat at attention and listened to how her cherished life came crumbling down around her, through no real fault of her own.

Her new start-up was doing well until her husband broke his back at work. He was permanently disabled, and all the financial burden fell on her shoulders.

Needing more income and the benefits her self-employment didn't offer, she gave up her company to work for Boeing. She rose to the top wage there as a woman in a man's world. That didn't bother her. She was used to being different. It was part of her recipe for success.

Eventually, something did bother her.

It was her feet. They started to break down from standing on cold concrete, working on airplane wings every day. She endured it without complaint. Just as she silently left the house at the crack of dawn, kissing her miracle of a son before she started the 90-minute morning commute to a job she hated. There was nothing offering this pay and benefits in the country near her farm.

She chose to be grateful.

She made another choice, which became the tipping point of her demise.

She needed to book an appointment with a podiatrist. Rather than selecting the top-rated surgeon with an office in the city, she chose the convenience of a local doctor she saw on the daily drive home. It was a medical malpractice disaster.

After 6 surgeries on both feet, she could no longer stand, walk or work. How was she to care for her toddler and disabled husband? Boeing let her go; she drained her savings and lost her home, her prized horses, and all the animals. Add to this, the devastation of losing her mother.

For a while they were homeless, sleeping near the railroad tracks with a 2-year-old. With nowhere else to go, they drove 3,335 miles in a patched-up pick-up truck and dog kenneled on the flatbed to live in a 10x12 bedroom with her estranged father.

But this was no free ride. Desperate for income and food, she took a cashier job at a grocery store, standing for 8 hours per day. The physical pain from her feet, the emotional abuse from her father, and the shame of losing everything brought her to her knees.

It also brought her back to me.

She sounded broken beyond repair. It was all too much tragedy for her. The single thread that kept her clinging to life was her son, DJ. He was her miracle birth; the child she was told she could never have.

Reluctantly, I asked, "How can I help you?"

"I read your book, SOAR. As I was reading it, something was changing in my brain. I can't explain it. But I know you can help me. I want what you did in that book.

Writing is my great passion. I also worked with therapeutic clients for 12 years after getting my PhD, but she was too far gone for me to treat. I had shifted to business clients. She couldn't afford me.

I politely declined.

She begged.

I defended myself.

She begged. And begged. And begged some more.

And in her begging, she started to become THAT Angie again. She was a fighter. And she was going to be the hero, the Noah of her family once again.

It would be a steep climb back.

At that point, she felt like an orphan, had a 453 FICO, massive debt, no home, a vaccine-afflicted toddler, a disabled husband in chronic pain equal to her own, and frightful night terrors from psychotherapy quackery.

On the plus side, she had a sister who told her to apply to college so she could get student loans. With that and her income from Walmart, we worked together on her consciousness for a year, using The SOAR Formula.

She came into The Academy in the worst place of any client I ever had

...and came out as the best.

When people ask her why she is so happy and why it worked for her, she always has the same answer.

"SOAR changed my life and saved my life. I just followed the 4 steps."

At the end of that year, she came to me and said, now I want to start my own business again.

I told her if she follows the same 4 steps in business, she will hit 6 figures in a year.

She laughed, and said, "No way."

Even though she had to have an emergency life-saving surgery that left her bedridden for 2 months, her company reached the 6-figure mark in 6 months by being Noah to the rest of the world. This summer she graduated magna cum laude and is starting her MBA in the fall. She is committed to a 4.0 GPA.

Angie has become a true hero to her clients, her family, and me.

While I could help keep one hero on this planet, thousands more heroes fought for our freedom around the world and have come home without the strength or resources to fight for their lives.

Our military has become devastated by the physical and psychological effects of war. They have done their part, now it's time for each of us to do ours.

Find a way to go two-by-two with a heroic veteran and inspire them to live another day.

The world needs more Noahs.

Meet The Author:

Koni Scavella is an international speaker, 3-time #1 best-selling author, and business growth strategist for CEOs and entrepreneurs seeking quantum leaps in their lives and business simultaneously. She also hosts the SOAR to Freedom podcast and the weekly show, Iconic TV Live.

Dr. Koni Scavella has the rare gift of combining science and the arts to form a powerful recipe for success in business. With over 20 years in film and fashion, C-Suite Consulting, and building 5 multi-million-dollar companies starting from scratch, she is driven to help today's entrepreneurs simplify, systemize, and scale their businesses in record breaking time.

She has worked with new start-ups, Fortune 500 and Inc 500 companies in healthcare, real estate, coaching, education, sports, finance, oil and gas, retail, ministry, hospitality, and entertainment.

Koni's life and career have traversed the globe. Born in Munich, Germany, she also speaks 5 languages.

The turning point for her came when she was diagnosed with terminal cancer twice. While she healed from both without any medical intervention, surgery or chemotherapy, the transformational Near-Death encounter following the second diagnosis is what shapes her life's mission today.

With advanced degrees in physics, theology and business, Koni is a true pioneer with her research in the advancement of human consciousness and disruptive business design. By blending her passion for the latest discoveries inneuroscience, quantum physics, psychology, medicine, and spirituality with her profound Near-Death experience, she brings a fresh approach to her speaking, writing and business mentorship.

Using her proprietary 4-square methodologies, The SOAR Formula, The Celebrity Factor, The Iconic Blitz Method, PNI, The Oasis Method, and 21-Day Mind Mastery System, Koni's clients DOUBLE their results in HALF the time...having twice the fun.

Her other best-selling books include SOAR: Think Bigger, Move Faster, Rise Higher, The Power of a Wish: How to Attract Anything You Desire, and the soon to be published, Beyond Mindset. Invite Koni to speak at your event or call to work with her privately or join her Iconic Leadership Academy to take your business from 6-figures to 7-figures in one year.

Her company, The Iconic Brands, is composed of The Iconic Entrepreneur, a free group that teaches 7-figure strategies, The Iconic VA, The Iconic Design Group,

Iconic Publishing, Iconic Investments, Iconic Consulting and the newest all-in one software development, IconiSphere.

When she is not buried in books, you can find Koni with her toes buried in the sand near her home in Del Mar, California.

To inquire about hiring Koni to speak, to work with her privately, or to join her Iconic Leadership Academy, go to Koni Scavella.com, TheIconicEntrepreneur.com or MeetKoni.com.

To read her books on Amazon or Audible, go to: KoniScavella.net

To listen to her podcast, go to: KoniScavella.org

Journey to the Light

By Paula Slavens

"I'm dying anyway; why don't we commit double suicide?" A journey to the light—and finding my WHY. Those words still ring in my ears, an echo of the time when my husband Rick and I faced our darkest hour. I still cringe when I think about them and the sense of despair that plummeted him to the level of even suggesting it.

From December 2007 to 2009, an economic collapse and recession affected the entire world. When you're small business owners with a discretionary type product, that's double jeopardy because people naturally click into survival modes and limit expenditures. A thriving business can suddenly become a barren desert.

If you add years of illness, a prognosis of impending death, and mounting medical bills, that level of hardship can suck the breath right out of you and spiral you into a sense of hopelessness. Your brain feels like mush, your stomach like an acid bath eating you from the inside out.

The day the letter arrived from the mortgage company left a crystal-clear imprint on my brain. Our lovely neighbor Laurie had stopped by to visit with Rick on the back patio overlooking our colorful English-style garden. A pleasantly warm summer day, filled with birdsong and sweet smells, suddenly seemed black, devoid of life and beauty. The words stuck in my throat as I read the letter conveying that our attempts at negotiations were over. We would have to vacate our beautiful home.

We had anticipated the clock would run out on Rick first, but our mortgage lender said the hour had arrived; they could no longer extend our stay. Laurie cried with us, prayed with us, and tried to assure us that somehow, it would be okay.

It wasn't. We had no place to go. Not only had our income dried up, but we had also depleted our savings, my inheritance, Rick's retirement fund, and most of mine as well. Rick's life insurance would help me rebuild my life; I just needed to hang on. Dipping into my resources seemed like the least I could do when Rick insisted this was the home where he wanted to die. My compelling need to honor his wishes ultimately proved to be a bad choice.

I now understand the level of desperation and defeat that causes people to commit suicide. At the same time, my age-old belief system screamed that it was a selfish act. Death would extinguish our pain, but family and friends would face a lifetime of grief and self-questioning. I couldn't do that to them. Somehow, I would figure out something. I would make it work. I had to! No—no matter how much trouble we faced—a double suicide was simply out of the question!

The power of prayer opens doors; perseverance and hard work allow you to march through them into a new beginning. However, before that could even happen, I needed to humble myself and ask for help. Being independent and working hard doesn't always guarantee success—you need to admit you need wise counsel, resources not within your grasp, and helping hands that can take over when exhaustion consumes you.

The heroes of my story are the people who helped us and changed that darkest hour into rays of hope and comfort. Family, friends, members of our church, and neighbors rallied behind us, providing badly needed helping hands, guidance, and support that I still attribute to an act of God.

Friends helped me box up our household, a neighbor took care of Rick—physically and emotionally—another friend rented a truck and rallied helpers for loading and unloading. One friend even cared for our house plants until we had a place to put them. However, before that all happened, we needed a miracle.

Have you ever thought that God brings people into your life when you truly need them? My person was Bev—a woman I had met just a couple of years earlier. She provided emotional support and made it her mission to find us a home—and she did. It was not our dream house, but it had potential; all one level, and by adding a ramp at the front entry, it would be exactly what we needed for Rick's limited mobility.

Realizing my only recourse was a lease-to-own arrangement, I prepared a proposal, which I shared with Bev, and she copied it to her parents. At the appointed meeting time with the realtor and homeowners, both Bev and her parents met us at the house.

After a brief discussion, the homeowner adamantly declared he wanted only a conventional sale. I suddenly felt the same as the day we received our notice from the mortgage company. I choked back tears and struggled to find my voice—my stomach in a vice grip. We were running out of time. I needed a home—one where Rick could find peace for his remaining days. It wouldn't be the home where he wanted to die, but it would be a roof over our heads. Thoughts of Rick's suicide suggestion flooded my thoughts. What can I do? All hope felt suddenly extinguished. Then I heard the voice of Bev's father from the other side of the room, "What if we bought the house?"

Rick and I looked at each other in disbelief. How could that be? We hardly knew these people. The rest of the details remain a blur to me, as I sat there in shock. A rushing wind seemed to fill my ears, and I could hear nothing but the beat of my heart. Rick would be safe. We would have a home. Bev's parents would become our landlords and honor the lease-to-own agreement we so desperately needed. The house was ours. That was our miracle—the path toward the light—hope triumphing over certain doom!

It wasn't anything like the beautiful home we had to vacate. In fact, neighbors described it as the worst house on the block—badly in need of repairs and major yard cleanup with 50 dandelions growing in the patchy front lawn. The moss on the roof looked healthier than the grass, and the muddy backyard contained debris from house repairs and abandoned garden projects. Upgrades made before putting the house on the market were poor quality and even more poorly installed—the proverbial lipstick on a pig!

It was also half the size of our home, making it difficult to find enough space for everything. That lack of space proved to be the hardest part of the move—and I didn't realize how bad it was until I opened the garage door. I was met with a wall of boxes—floor to ceiling. Remember the closing scene of Raiders of the Lost Ark? It was like that but with no neat aisleways—just boxes!

Fatigue consumed every ounce of my being, and I succumbed to a complete meltdown. Rick was asleep, and I could just cry my eyes out without causing anyone grief. It felt horrible—yet good—a release of pent-up worry, grief, and utter exhaustion.

After pulling myself together, I excavated boxes, stacking them in the living room and creating a narrow path that snaked its way to the corner of the room where our new internet service would be installed the following day. When we were children growing up on a dairy farm, we did that with hay bales—creating tunnels to lead us into little rooms dotted throughout the hay barn. Of course, this endeavor lacked any fun and adventure—but when the technician arrived, he could complete his work, ensuring we had internet service.

More answers to prayers—solutions to a brighter world!

We had a place to live. How to live became the next issue, as I faced the daunting task of caring for Rick along with organizing our new home, making improvements, and earning an income.

My sister Jan proved to be my latest hero. As a retired registered nurse, she helped our mother when she was dying. She cared for her husband when he gave up the will to live after a stroke— and she moved in with us to help make Rick's end days more manageable.

179

Jan also plunged into home improvement projects and yard work. Ol' farm girls can accomplish a lot in a few short years. With help from skilled craftsmen, we transformed the house into a home now described as the best on our street. In fact, it's become my favorite of all the places I've lived.

Rick is gone. With the passage of time, the sting is less bitter, while good memories remain in your heart forever. A partner and soulmate can never be replaced—but life with my widowed sister is a good arrangement. Our shared history eliminates a lot of need for explanation, our similarities make decisions easier, and our differences provide checks and balances, as well as fresh ideas. We are also not averse to changing our minds thirty times before coming up with the perfect solution—something that used to drive Rick nuts.

Finding my why.

These past years have not been easy, and I shudder at what could have transpired—were it not for the heroes who so richly blessed us.

All of my contemporaries are now retired, and Jan often asks, "Why aren't you satisfied with just making do? Why are you pursuing a new career when most people your age would just give up?"

The answer is easy. After experiencing those Dickens' words, "It was the worst of times," finding my why is the desire to create abundance and share my successes with others. I want to give back and be a hero to others who have reached their critical limits and need financial support.

My reason also includes setting up income streams for all sixteen of my nieces and nephews, paying for my youngest nephew's education so he can fulfill his dream of becoming a doctor, and ensuring that my five siblings can live worry-free as we face our end days. Beyond meeting these personal and family goals, my why includes reaching out to communities to help end homelessness. People lost homes during the pandemic, and scientists predict we have not seen the last of plague-like illnesses. No one should be in a position to consider giving up life as the best solution.

There is always a way—sometimes a miracle is someone who says, let me help.

Meet The Author:

Paula Slavens

If you've ever been told, "You ought to write a book," we made it happen. We—included an entrepreneurial business as the husband-and-wife team of Rick and Paula Slavens, with U.S. clients ranging from the Pacific Northwest to the East Coast and southern states of Florida and Georgia. As an award-winning graphic designer, writer, videographer, and skilled interviewer, Paula combined her skills with Rick's extensive research, marketing, and genealogy expertise. Together, they created projects that included personal, family, and company books, videos, posters, and even historical wall murals for museums and family residences.

After Rick's untimely death, Paula decided to make a career change that wouldn't require travel, offer multiple revenue streams, and have growth potential without the labor-intensive creative demands of old. That led her down the path of digital marketing and now affiliate marketing.

Even though affiliate marketing is a new venture for Slavens, her level of expertise is visible in two other businesses she has developed.

Video Marketing: personalizedvideoads.com

Referral Marketing: pva-testimonials.com

"Whereas my work in the past benefitted the few, my new career brings business and wealth opportunities to the masses," says Slavens.

Keep your eyes open for Paula Slavens. She aims to make a difference!

LinkedIn: https://www.linkedin.com/in/paula-slavens-pva/

If You Were Going to Die Tomorrow...

By Rob Wallace

If You were going to die tomorrow, how much would you be willing to pay to restore your health and live an extra 20 years?

How would that extra 20 years impact your business life and decision making?

This question is one that thousands of entrepreneurs have considered over the past 30 years. It is a question that has led them to completely re-examine their assumptions about their business and life.

Research suggests that retirement is bad for your health. Many people start to go downhill in the second year of retirement.

A lack of purpose contributes to mental decline, and when combined with social isolation, and often leads to depression which affect the physical health, creating a vicious cycle.

What is the alternative approach?

Dan Sullivan is busy mapping out the next 78 years of his life. That kind of long-term planning is hard to fathom. What is more remarkable is that he is 78 years old now.

Dan is a "quick start" an attribute that has made him successful coach of entrepreneurs. His programs start out by challenging participants to imagine that they will live a healthy life for decades longer than they imagined. It challenges them to examine their fundamental assumptions about their business and life.

Dan is a biohacker - his home is stacked with a range of high-tech equipment that

pushes his body to the limit.

Steven Kotler is another bio hacker. His passion for extreme sports led him to become obsessed with the state of flow. A prolific author on peak performance, he started the Flow Research Collective to advance the understanding of peak performance.

His research has led him to understand that peak performance comes from getting our biology to work for us not against us. He states, "Personality doesn't scale only biology scales." Being able to perform at our best requires cognitive literacy. Understanding what is going on in our bodies and mind. Thinking takes place in your brain and body.

As an extreme skier, he noticed that some of the best skiers on the hardest

Get $1,567 in Bonuses at www.EveryDayHeroesBook.com

mountains were significantly older than him and impossible to beat. He began to question his assumptions about aging. One thing that intrigued him was how Antonio Stradivari seemed to get better as the master craftsman of the world's most valuable musical instruments. He made two of the most valued violins when he was 92 years old in 1737.

A conversation with the late Mihaly Csikszentmihalyi the founder of Flow Psychology crystallized his need to explore peak performance aging. He has discovered aging is not what you think it is. Lifelong learning is the core of peak performance aging.

His insights include:

Almost everything we thought about aging is wrong.

We are capable of things in the later part of our lives that no one thought

possible 20 years ago.

We have opportunities to unlock cognitive superpowers for lifelong learning.

We have a ton of untapped economic performance in the second half our lives.

Aging is a mental game. It helps to start young but it's never too late to start.

Both men collaborate with futurist Peter Diamandis, best known for his X-Prize Foundation. Dan and Peter share their wisdom on the Exponential Wisdom podcast. While Peter and Steven wrote Abundance, Bold and The Future is Faster Than You Think.

Peter studied medicine at Harvard and MIT, but he had already caught the entrepreneurial bug. He became interested in space travel. By the time that he was finishing his studies in medicine, he was already running two companies.

Like many great entrepreneurs, Peter took an idea that had previously been applied and made it better. He was inspired by the Orteig Prize that led to the first non-stop flight between New York and Paris. He started to Ansari XPrize a $10 Million for the first private 3-man space craft to achieve 2 flights that went 100 km into space within 2 weeks.

The XPRIZE model had proved its value. The Ansari XPRIZE paved the way for private enterprise led development of space to benefit the world. Elon Musk's SPACEX and Starlink are prime examples.

Not content with redefining space exploration and development, he committed his organization to solving other global problems. Global education gaps, water scarcity, ocean oil spills etc. and now the disease of aging.

Peter views retirement for men as synonymous with rapid aging. Though, he sees aging as a disease that can be treated.

Perhaps the world's most famous biohacker is a 62-year-old man who puts his body through extreme challenges and he has a pit crew that works with Formula One precision to keep him on the track. His events attract tens of thousands of participants who find his events life changing.

His course offerings and books have evolved with his personal focus. He has evolved from empowerment, health, entrepreneurship and business growth to investment and wealth and now his focus has moved to longevity.

His most recent book Life Force outlines the developments in longevity technology that makes it all possible. When he writes a book, he identifies the top hundred leaders in the domain and sets out to interview them all. For this book Tony Robbins engaged his friends Peter Diamandis and Bob Hariri, the neurosurgeon and stem cell expert.

The three of them are investing heavily in making the cutting-edge life extension technologies available to the public. Opening Fountain Life Clinics around the US and looking to expand around the world in the near future. The Fountain Life approach uses proactive testing and treatments provided through extraordinary concierge medical clinics.

Fountain Life is using the Grail blood test that detect cancer at early stages. It can detect a wide range of cancers well before symptoms appear. They combine it with full body MRI, DEXA bone scans, metal toxicity tests, heart scans, genomic and nutragenomic tests, DNA age and methylation tests to gain a full picture of how their patients are aging. Enabling them to work out the best way to reverse the aging process.Fountain Life represents what they view as the best way to deliver health care rather than "sick care."

Their book provides a broad overview of the breakthroughs that have occurred in treating aging and age-related disease. They provide a wide range of accessible and actionable advice on age reversal.

The important question that it answers is how you can add 20 years or more of vitality into your life?

Are you ready to embrace the opportunity live a bigger future?
For more information go to www.robsfreegift.com/lifeextension

Meet The Author:

 Rob Wallace is an investor based in Sydney, Australia.

He helps engineering services business owners scale and exit. The demographic shift of ageing baby boomers business owners is the biggest challenge in this sector.

He has been in the agricultural, manufacturing and distribution sectors. He has worked in startups and multi-generational family businesses. So he understands the challenges of the business lifecycle.

Having grown up in an entrepreneurial family, he has always sought to learn from leading thinkers in business and technology.

One Little Word Can Bring Time and Energy

By Mr. X

The ability to say no is a critical life skill.

Unfortunately, many people never learn how to properly say no, and as a result they miss out on opportunities, get taken advantage of, and generally fail to reach their full potential in life.

Here are four reasons why you should start saying no more often:

1. Saying No Helps You Prioritize Your Time and Energy

If you're constantly saying yes to everything, you're going to spread yourself too thin and end up exhausted.

It's important to be selective with your time and energy and only invest them in things that are truly important to you. Otherwise, you'll just end up wasting your time on things that don't matter.

2. Saying No Gives You a Sense of Control

When you're constantly saying yes to other people, you're essentially handing over control of your life.

You're letting other people dictate how you spend your time, what you do with your energy, and where your focus should be.

Instead of living someone else's life, start taking control by saying no more often. This way, you can direct your own life and make choices that are in alignment with your own values and goals.

3. Saying No Makes You More Assertive

Saying no is an assertive act. It shows that you're confident in your ability to make decisions and that you're not afraid to stand up for yourself.

If you're not used to being assertive, it might feel uncomfortable at first. But the more you practice saying no, the easier it will become. And as you become more assertive, you'll find that other areas of your life will improve as well.

4. Saying No Can Help You Achieve Your Goals

If your goal is to get ahead in your career, for example, then saying no to social invitations and other time-wasting activities will free up more time for you to focus on your work.

In general, learning how to say no can help you achieve any goal because it allows you to direct your time and energy towards things that are actually important to you.

Saying no isn't always easy, but it's a skill that's worth learning. Start practicing today and you'll soon see the benefits in your own life.

Meet The Author:

When I was asked for my bio, I said NO.

I want to be known as Mr. X. Look, I'm considered by many to be one of the top online marketers. No one has ever met in person or ever will. I like it that way. I enjoy people not knowing who I am because I like to play in highly competitive markets online which means I have a line of competitors just waiting to knock me off.

That is why I'd like to keep my identity secret and also why I would like to keep my niche secret. I hope you can respect that. Never forget that one little two letter word I wrote about. It truly can bring you time and energy.

189

6 Life Lessons from Owning Elderly Care Homes for Over 27 Years

By Harvey Zemmel

I bought my first residential care home for the elderly [assisted living centers for our American friends] in the United Kingdom back in 1995.

I have owned and operated both individual care homes where I have been the sole owner and a group of 10 care homes, which I owned with investors. I currently own and operate 2 care homes. I have reflected, and these are the 6 life lessons I can draw on from my experience.

Greater Medical Advances Bring Greater Complexity

When I had my first care home, residents primarily came into our homes for social, not medical, reasons. They were isolated and lonely. We provided a new stimulating social environment and they stayed for many years.

In some instances, back in 1995, we referred to a few of our residents as 'pleasantly confused.' This was the language we used. Time has moved on, and we now know these residents had Alzheimer's or other types of dementia. A new language has come with ever-increasing knowledge.

The Alzheimer's Society was only formed in April 1980 to unite caregivers, provide support to those facing Alzheimer's, and advance research into the disease. There are now 55 million people worldwide who have this disease, and this number is growing at an alarming rate. Today, the revenue for the US Alzheimer's Society [$400m] and the United Kingdom Alzheimer's Society [£111m] allows them to educate the world.

It is not only language and education that have progressed. We are living longer, and medicine is a major contributory factor to the extension of our lives. However, our residents come into our homes with more challenging and complex physical, medical, and emotional issues. We look after the most vulnerable in our society – we don't make widgets in a factory. Now more than ever, there is an even greater responsibility to understand and respond to our residents who are entering their new homes with these complex care needs.

Increasing Consumer Expectations Create Greater Opportunities for Reputational Damage. There was no TripAdvisor, Facebook, or other social media back in 1995.

If as a consumer you have a poor experience, not only do you tell your friends, but you now post your experience on TripAdvisor and social media. We have all become more educated and our expectations for that service have become significantly greater, whether it be in our local Italian restaurant or the hotel we visit on our vacation. It is no different when looking after elderly people. This is fine but I have just outlined earlier that our residents have complex care needs, so there is a greater risk for reputational damage.

Amazing Staff Team

I remember in the middle of the pandemic here in the United Kingdom on a Thursday evening at 8.00 pm, people would go outside and spontaneously clap for the National Health Service [NHS]. Many people gathered in the streets all around the United Kingdom to show their appreciation for people working in the hospitals as they were saving lives.

This was very laudable, but what about the other healthcare professionals in social care? We were working equally hard, saving the lives of our vulnerable residents in the storm of the pandemic.

The social care workforce throughout the world has always been undervalued by governments and societies. This group of people is paid minimum wage rates, yet they are expected to provide compassionate and professional care for our mums and dads.

This group of people has a choice of where to work, as they could stack the shelves of the local Tesco or Walmart for a similar wage. However, they feel a greater need to care and contribute in a meaningful way to society. They're loyal, committed, and care for our residents as if they were their own mum, grandma, or aunt. I have been privileged to work with this group of dedicated people. They are true heroes.

100-Year-Olds Still Have Needs and Desires

I remember in my second year in business we had a resident who was approaching 100 years old. Her mind was still sharp. We asked her what she would like to do to celebrate her birthday. We were astonished by her reply. 'I want a Strip gram.' The home was split as half the staff was shocked and appalled, and the other half thought 'good for her!' Her daughter was in the shocked and appalled corner. I agreed to her request. It was naturally done tastefully and sensitively. She, and the rest of the residents, had a memorable afternoon [yes...she survived the experience!].

Our residents not only have lived full lives before they came into their new homes, but they have their own needs and desires. They can still live a different but fulfilled life in a care home. We often forget or neglect this critical point.

Expect the Unexpected

I have been in this business for 27 years, but nothing could have prepared me, and my staff team, for the Covid pandemic.

In the United Kingdom, there were 45,000 care home covid deaths [22% of all covid deaths]. In America, there were 200,000 care home deaths [20% of all covid deaths].

We were living a daily nightmare. In the first wave, we lost 16 residents in 6 weeks in one home. In the second wave, we lost 9 residents in 4 weeks in our other home. It was traumatic...every day.

I was having to make decisions about life and death at the peak, often on an hourly basis. The complexity and intensity were relentless for all of us.

My experience did help, and there were two things that I did which, on reflection, assisted everyone.

I led from the front. I was there every day alongside my staff teams in both waves. We experienced the trauma together.

Second, communication was key, as we communicated weekly [even when we had bad news to deliver] to our families and other stakeholders.

Forever Learning

No day is the same and, even after 27 years, part of the joy is each week getting asked new questions from my staff team about situations I have not encountered before.

It may be related to my staff team. I have managed large staff teams of over 500, but currently, my staff team is 85. That is still a significant responsibility.

In recent years, a staff member has suffered the trauma of their young daughter passing away. We are currently supporting a staff member who has a terminal illness. Notwithstanding my legal responsibilities as their employer, what can I, and my staff team, constructively do to support these people?

It may be related to our residents.

I have seen the best and worst in humanity particularly at the time of a resident passing away.

What happens when a father and daughter have been estranged for many years and the father expressly wants that to remain? At the time the resident becomes seriously ill and is on end-of-life care do we contact the daughter or honor the wishes of the father? What about the funeral...do we contact the daughter?

193

We face these, and other moral dilemmas, regularly. There are no right and wrong answers. It depends on your own moral compass.

I am no hero. My staff team members are true heroes, as we do the very best for our residents, as that is where our responsibility lies.

Meet The Author:

Harvey Zemmel has successfully owned and operated elderly care homes [assisted living centers for our American friends] in the United Kingdom. He and his team have won industry awards for their contribution.

Further, Harvey Zemmel is the founder of All About Alzheimer's which is a membership site for caregivers whose loved ones have Alzheimer's or other dementias.

All About Alzheimer's shares the latest news, developments, solutions, advice and tips to its caregivers' members – see www.allaboutalzheimers.com

How To Get Over $1,567 In Bonuses

Simply follow 3 steps on this page:

>>> www.EveryDayHeroesBook.com <<<

On behalf of all co-authors in this book, thank you again for getting Everyday Heroes 3.

Remember, 100% of ALL royalties for this book will be donated to Habitat for Humanity!

Made in the USA
Las Vegas, NV
18 November 2022

59729001R00109